Oct. 6, 2006

Joint Custody with a Jerk: Raising a Child with an Uncooperative Ex

JOINT
CUSTODY
WITH A
*Jerk**

*jerk\ˈjərk\ *n* **1** an ex-wife or ex-husband who continually annoys you with stupid, irrational, and immature behavior **2** one whose values differ so dramatically from yours that you wonder how you will ever make it through your child's lifetime

Raising a Child with an Uncooperative Ex

Julie A. Ross, M.A., and Judy Corcoran

St. Martin's Press
New York

JOINT CUSTODY WITH A JERK: RAISING A CHILD WITH AN UNCOOPERATIVE EX.
Copyright © 1996 by Julie A. Ross & Judy Corcoran. All rights reserved.
Printed in the United States of America. No part of this book may be used
or reproduced in any manner whatsoever without written permission
except in the case of brief quotations embodied in critical articles or re-
views. For information, address St. Martin's Press, 175 Fifth Avenue,
New York, N.Y. 10010.

Book design by Richard Oriolo

Library of Congress Cataloging-in-Publication Data

Ross, Julie A.
    Joint custody with a jerk : raising a child with an uncooperative
    ex / by Julie A. Ross and Judy Corcoran.—1st ed.
      p. cm.
    ISBN 0-312-14113-0
    1. Children of divorced parents. 2. Joint custody of children.
  3. Divorced parents. 4. Parenting, Part-time. I. Corcoran, Judy.
  HQ777.5.R66 1996
  306.89—dc20   95-47288
                                            CIP

To my supportive husband, Steve, for his unwavering belief in me, and for his insight and intelligence, which have made our parenting partnership so rewarding.

To my daughter, Emilie, and her friend, Rebecca, for their patience and resourcefulness in occupying themselves while I wrote.

To my son, Daniel, for his blissfully long naps at all the right times.

—J. A. R.

To my terrific daughter, Molly, for her unending patience and love, and to Craig Baumunk, Peter Thall, and Susan Bristol for their constant support and friendship.

—J. C.

Contents

Joint Custody with a Jerk: Raising a Child with an Uncooperative Ex

Introduction

When my husband rolled over twelve years ago and said, "Let's have a baby," it never occurred to me that, five years later, I would be standing in the back of a crowded and hot auditorium, alone, watching my daughter tap-dance her heart out, only to find her father and his new wife sitting in the third row.

Nor did I imagine that I would be celebrating Thanks-giving one week early because my daughter would be spending the fourth Thursday in November with her father at her new stepgrandmother's house. And I certainly never planned to raise a child as a single parent and to battle with my ex-husband over nearly every small detail and large issue of our daughter's life.

I sometimes envy those couples who can divorce and say "Good-bye and good luck!" and whose biggest divorce-related problem is who gets the Billy Joel CDs. When a child is part of your divorce, your involvement with your ex-spouse is often forever, or at least until your child graduates from school or marries. In those one to ninety-nine years, there will be countless ballet recitals, school meetings, soccer games, birthday parties, proms, weddings, funerals, and so on, in which your child will want both parents to attend or participate and about which you and your ex-spouse will discuss, disagree, negotiate, battle, ignore, argue, and sometimes, in the tradition of true jerks, *intentionally* annoy each other.

The idea for *Joint Custody with a Jerk* came about through a need I experienced as a divorced mother and a relationship I developed with Julie Ross.

Julie Ross is a family counselor with a private practice, a writer, and a parent educator. Both my daughter and I saw her a few times for counseling around the time my ex-husband was remarrying. I was immediately fascinated by Julie's demeanor and the way she related to my daughter.

Sometime later I ran into Julie walking on the street with her young daughter, Emilie. While we were exchanging hellos, Emilie pulled away from Julie and began to run off down the sidewalk. Julie quickly caught hold of her and looked her directly in the eyes and said, "Emilie, when you run away from me, I feel very nervous because this is a crowded sidewalk. Please hold my hand and stay with me." I was amazed to see Emilie settle right down. I was intrigued with their relationship, which seemed to be based on respect, cooperation, and responsibility.

I asked Julie about the technique she had just used with Emilie, and she told me that it was one of the communication techniques that she teaches in her nine-week parenting seminar. I signed up right there.

During the next nine weeks, I saw the benefit that these proven techniques might have if I used them on my ex-husband. At the time, we were barely speaking. If these techniques worked on an eight-year-old, I said to Julie, wouldn't they work on someone I believed to have the maturity of an eight-year-old? She confirmed that they most certainly would.

Around this same time, I was befriending a lot of single parents, both dads and moms. I heard story after story about what jerks their ex-spouses could be at times. One friend was beside himself because he had just found out that his ex was leaving their six-year-old child alone while she went to the supermarket. My friends told me about scheduling problems, value differences, lost possessions, and dietary restrictions, and about immaturity, uncooperation, manipulation, and irresponsibility. It seemed that no one knew about or used the communication skills that Julie taught and that there were few self-help books written for parents raising a child with an uncooperative ex. I saw a real need for professional guidance.

I approached Julie about collaborating on a book that would frame these techniques (plus many others) in the joint-custody scenario. She shared my enthusiasm, and we began working together: learning, researching, writing, fine-tuning, and applying the various communication skills on some real-life situations. We immediately saw what a difference practical communication skills can make. Thus, through the experiences of Julie's clients and through the stories and experiences of my single-parent friends, we developed a model for handling communication challenges with a jerk.

From the beginning, when either of us mentioned the title of this book, people chuckled and said, "I bet it will be hilarious." Unfortunately, there's nothing funny about raising a child with an uncooperative ex. In most divorces, everyone suffers at some point. Although we try to keep it light, the subject matter of this book is *not* humorous. Once you hear a child cry for his or her other parent after returning home from a weekend visit, a little piece of your heart breaks off.

Julie and I wrote this book to appeal to many people, not just newly divorced mothers and fathers. Even among those who have been sharing custody for years, new situations arise where every drop of cooperation is needed to raise happy and healthy children. And the health and happiness of our children is truly the goal here.

Although we are women, the jerks we write about are not always men. Because everyone can be a jerk at times, we alternate genders throughout the book.

Both Julie and I would like to thank the many people who helped make this book possible by supporting our ideas and sharing their stories with us. We would especially like to thank our agent, Bob Levine, for leading us through this process, and our editor, Jennifer Weis, whose persistence launched this book and whose enthusiasm and genuine love for the subject of parenting are inspirational.

—JUDY CORCORAN

What Did I Ever See in My Ex?

"Every time my ex breaks up with a man, she goes to bed for a few days. That leaves our five-year-old daughter virtually unattended. My daughter doesn't get outside to play, she misses birthday parties, and she just lies around the house watching television because of this woman's sick behavior."

"My son thinks his dad can do no wrong. But my ex lies to us all the time. He says he can't pick up our son on Saturday morning because he has to work. When I call his office to offer to drop Danny off, he's not there. It makes me crazy!"

"My ex is constantly changing her plans and then expects me to change mine. I'm really tired of it. But what can I do? If my ex cancels visitation at the last minute, I can't leave the kids alone."

"My ex thinks it's perfectly safe to leave our eight-year-old daughter alone. He leaves her alone in his apartment, in stores, in the car, everywhere. I just go nuts when I think of the danger involved."

"This summer, I planned to take my son to the beach for two weeks in August. My ex-wife found out and took him to the same beach for two weeks in July. By the time August came, my son said he was tired of the beach and wouldn't go with me. I could kill my ex for undermining my plans."

"When the kids go to visit their father for the weekend, it's party time. He feeds them junk, lets them stay up all night to watch R-rated movies, and has no regard for their personal hygiene. Late Sunday night, he returns them sick, tired, and dirty. I have a terrible time getting them up for school on Monday."

"My ex never bothers to repack my daughter's clothes, schoolwork, games, etc., so that we always have a big scene when she returns home and realizes that she's missing these things. I'm really tired of buying new hats, dolls, and sweatshirts because her dad can't remember to pack them."

"Not only does my ex put our ten-year-old daughter to bed at seven-thirty on Saturday night with his three- and two-year-olds, I just found out that he locks them in the bedroom to keep the babies from getting out of bed. Isn't that a fire hazard? What if our daughter has to go to the bathroom in the middle of the night? I don't know how I can, in good conscience, let her visit there again."

"Whenever our son gets even a minor illness, my ex starts rearranging the visitation plans. It's as if she doesn't want him to spend the night, or have contact with her new husband, but she still wants to see him. So she'll call me sounding desperate and ask if she can just take him for the day, to the zoo or to the park, and return him before dinner. Or she'll ask if she can take him for a few hours to a movie instead of overnight. I really think her new husband is behind this. He's got a high-powered job and seems absolutely paranoid about getting sick and missing work. I want my ex to see our son, and she does too, but one time she even wanted me to rearrange visitation because I mentioned that our son had athlete's foot."

Sharing Custody with a Jerk

Do you find that your ex has no respect for your time schedule, for the values you've worked so hard to instill in your child, and for the lifestyle you've developed with your child? Does your ex sometimes act or respond in immature, inconsiderate, and irresponsible ways? Is he or she, at times, a complete jerk?

If you are raising a child with an uncooperative ex, these scenarios most likely ring true in some form or another. In fact, if your ex husband or wife is a true jerk, you can probably add a few outrageous stories of your own. But whether you're dealing with an ex who intentionally tries to manipulate you and your child, or one who inadvertently confuses and complicates your life, there is help. This book offers simple yet effective tools to help you communicate with your ex, whether he or she is an occasional or a chronic jerk. These techniques will change how your ex reacts and responds to you. Instead of fighting and arguing about raising your child, you will soon be discussing and negotiating your child's future.

Using joint custody scenarios throughout this book, we demonstrate how these communication tools and techniques will help you solve problems and bring about changes in your relationship with your ex and your child. We revisit the problems mentioned at the beginning of this chapter as they apply in the later chapters. You should be able to substitute the details of your own particular problems into the structures we have set up to decide which course of action is best for you.

Life's Most Important Job

Raising a child is one of life's most important and difficult tasks. Yet most people undertake this enormous job with little or no experience or instruction. Most people, points out Terence T. Gorski, author of *Getting Love Right*, have had more training in how to drive a car than in how to parent a child or to conduct intimate relationships. Even fewer people are prepared to raise a child and negotiate the minute details of that child's future with someone for whom they've lost complete respect—an ex spouse who can, at times, be uncooperative and immature. Very few people would volunteer for a job like this!

And beyond this, even fewer people know instinctively how to teach responsibility to a child, or how to build self-esteem and instill values in their children in a world that is constantly changing. A large part of this book deals with just these things. You'll learn how to listen (as opposed to just waiting for your turn to talk), negotiate (uncover win/win alternatives), teach responsibility (to your ex and your child), take responsibility yourself (without taking on the problems of others), and foster cooperation among the three (or more) of you.

All of these, you'll discover, are crucial elements that will ensure that you and your child survive and thrive in the aftermath of your divorce.

Your Child Needs You

Study after study on divorce says that your child will turn out okay if you don't ask her to choose between you and your ex and if you provide her with a stable home life. But if you are like most parents in the throes of a divorce, stability might not be your strong suit right now. That's why it is beneficial for you to learn and use specific techniques that will enable you to handle situations with your ex in such a way that your child isn't damaged during this unstable period of your life.

The Scope of This Book

This book deals with change. In it, we present clear, practical techniques that, once you see the need for change, you can use to enact changes in yourself. Most of the time, the changes in your behavior will change your ex's behavior as well. However, if your ex is threatening you or your children with violence, you need to seek professional help. Exes who lose self-control are not just jerks. They have serious problems that the police and other authorities need to know about. Included in this category is constant verbal battering, which can be as damaging and hurtful as broken bones. An ex who engages in this kind of behavior is not within the scope of this book.

Nor do we deal with deadbeat moms and dads. We define deadbeats as those parents who physically, emotionally, and financially abandon their children. If your ex has run off, there are legal channels to follow. Laws are getting tougher every day in every state, but it is still an uphill battle to track down a deadbeat, and you have our sympathy.

You'll find that we present only one person's point of view in each example. We realize that there are two sides to every story, but if your jerk were willing to discuss your parenting and divorce issues with a therapist or counselor, these problems would be on their way to being solved.

This book is for the person who has no hope that his or her ex will even acknowledge that there's a problem, for the person who feels very alone in this coparenting situation. We've written it for those of you who are ready and willing to make the changes necessary to be effective and resourceful in dealing with the problems that arise from having joint custody with a jerk.

If It Walks Like a Jerk . . .

Many divorced parents get bogged down in guilt, as if they could have avoided the breakup. But wallowing in guilt or blaming your ex for the failed relationship may in fact keep you from moving forward and getting on with your life. It's important to be able to look at the divorce in its proper perspective, acknowledging and accepting responsibility for mistakes when it's appropriate *and* knowing when something wasn't your fault. Divorce is usually a two-way street.

It took Karen three years of self-blame before she was able to view the roles she and her ex had played in the divorce in their proper perspective. Much of that time she blamed herself for their bad postmarriage relationship. She felt that her aggressiveness about custody arrangements had caused her ex to behave like a jerk. But as the months passed, he became even more distant and uncooperative. Time after time he called to cancel visitation at the last minute, or didn't show up at all. He forgot their son's birthday one year and almost never sent gifts or even visited on the major holidays. Recently, Karen had this revelation:

> *"When I tell my friends about my ex's behavior, not one of them sticks up for my ex. You know, that tells me something. If he walks like a jerk, and talks like a jerk, chances are, HE'S A JERK!"*

Respect: A Casualty of Divorce

At some point in your divorce, you may wonder what you ever saw in your ex. The behaviors you once thought were cute and harmless have now become irritating and unaccept-able. That passionate phrase, "Don't stop, don't stop!" has turned into, "Oh, please, not that again." Your "one and only soulmate" is now "a total jerk." Your "ideal woman" has become a "conniving bitch." That "hunk of a guy" is now a "stupid bastard."

When a marriage dissolves, respect for your spouse usu-ally diminishes or disappears. Your view of your ex can change dramatically, and you may no longer respect his or her opinion, knowledge, and judgment. You also may not trust your ex, especially if he or she has broken the bond of trust through behavior or words.

Trust and respect for your ex, which once allowed you, as a couple, to arrive at harmonious agreement, is crucial in negotiating life's daily routine. Without it, even the most serene of us are driven to occasional fury. While you may never get to the point where you respect or trust your ex again, *acting* respectfully (and keeping your eyes open) can go a long way toward creating a healthy divorce.

Keeping It in Perspective

Divorces are usually ugly. The basic process of taking every-thing that was "ours" and dividing it into "yours" and "mine" is a negative action. On a personal level, divorces consist of one of you telling the other that you don't want to be partners anymore. All the plans you made won't happen now. All the sacrifices you made don't count. The promises are broken, and in the middle of your life, you have to start over. Divorce also represents the end of the fantasy of living happily ever after, of having a "normal" family life, of growing old with your spouse. You may now wonder who will love you when you're old or sick, and if you will ever meet someone again. You may feel like used goods. And on top of all this, your ex is a jerk!

To keep the fact that your ex is a jerk in perspective, it's important to realize that everyone is capable of acting like a jerk at times. Your ex, your boss, your neighbor, your parents, and even you possess the necessary ingredients to earn the name "jerk." In this book, we define a jerk as someone who intentionally fouls up your plans, who doesn't think things through, and who's inconsiderate, either consciously or subconsciously. Jerks lie to you, blame you for things, don't follow through, and in general, irritate you. They're selfish, spineless, and sometimes just plain stupid.

"There's this guy in my office who is a real jerk. He snaps at everyone and has this condescending attitude, so everyone snaps back at him. No one likes him, and everyone avoids working with him. One day, I decided enough was enough. I just wasn't going to play his game anymore. Now, when he asks me a question, I give him a straight answer and ignore his tone of voice or snide comments. I stopped wasting my time thinking up witty put-downs. And I noticed that he stopped snapping at me. He dropped his 'tough guy' attitude and now speaks to me normally. He's still a jerk with everyone else, but we definitely get along a lot better these days."

Admittedly, it's easier to deal with jerks when you have no emotional attachment to them. In all likelihood a coworker doesn't know you intimately and can't use that intimacy against you. But we all deal with jerks every day in every part of our lives. How to deal with them, rather than lamenting the fact that we must deal with them, is the issue. And the bottom line is that you can find happiness even if your ex is a jerk.

Your History Plays a Part

All people bring to their marriage the entire history of their relationships with their parents, siblings, and peers. Many therapists agree that the marital bed contains six people—you, your spouse, your parents, and your spouse's parents. The theory that we re-create in our marriage what felt familiar to us as children, whether it was healthy or not, is now generally accepted. It's like the old song says: "I want a girl just like the girl who married dear old dad." Ted's story about his initial meeting with Susan and the ensuing impact on his marriage illustrates this very point.

> *"When I met Susan on a blind date ten years ago, she was forty-five minutes late, and it didn't really bother me. She was all that I was looking for in a woman—beautiful, smart, high-powered, successful. Everything about her really turned me on. So what if she was late? She always had a good excuse like a traffic jam or a meeting at work. My mother was the same way. As a kid, I was always the last one to get picked up from baseball practice or to arrive at birthday parties. I guess I grew up thinking that women are just always late.*

"*During our marriage, Susan got a little better, but that was because I watched her very closely. If I saw her sitting down with a magazine at two-thirty when she was supposed to pick up Jimmy, our eight-year-old son, at three and he was a half hour away, I'd bring it to her attention. And if we were going out, I'd sometimes tell her that we had to be there at seven-thirty instead of eight, so if she started to run late, we would still get there on time.*

"*Over the years, though, her lack of regard for other people's schedules really began to bother me. And now that we're divorced, I can't put up with it anymore. She says she'll drop Jimmy off at one, so I make plans to go to a two-o'clock movie, and she shows up at two-ten. Or she says she'll pick him up at six and doesn't come until seven-thirty. By that time, he's hungry and wants to have dinner. Her lateness doesn't just affect me anymore, but it affects Jimmy, and sometimes my girlfriend and the baby-sitter.*

"*I don't know what I ever saw in Susan. She's so inconsiderate about time that it negates any good qualities she ever had. Obviously, there were other factors that contributed to our decision to divorce, but her being late was high on that list. I just have no respect for her anymore. And I find myself getting enraged just thinking about all the times I was late because of her. It's gotten to a point that I don't even want to discuss Jimmy's pickups and drop-offs with her. I put Jimmy on the phone and have him tell me what time she says she'll pick him up. And lately when she's late, he gets upset, and when I see him upset, I want to strangle her. I want to rip the hands off a clock and shove them down her throat.*"

It may sound odd that one of the reasons Ted was attracted to Susan when they first met was because she was late. But as he said, his mother was always late, and it was familiar to him. Terence T. Gorski says that the first time you marry, you marry your parents; the second time, you marry the opposite of your parents; and the third time, if you're lucky, you pick somebody you really like. Whether you're dealing with your first ex or a later ex, there's a bit of truth to the statement.

Ted admitted that Susan really turned him on. Gorski believes that your partners don't turn you on; you turn yourself on to them. You are first attracted to the similarities between yourself and the other person, which include looks, the sound of one's voice, and how one acts or reacts to a situation. You are next attracted to your complementary differences. The adage about opposites attracting is really more about being drawn to people who have the traits you admire, which are usually the traits you lack. You're attracted to the people who can help you move beyond your own limitations. That's how the organizer and the disorganized end up together. And finally, Gorski, as well as others, believe that people are attracted to the need to resolve their childhood conflicts. By trying to fix these conflicts with your spouse, you're actually trying to fix your parents.

If you came from a dysfunctional family (and many of us did), your need to resolve can result in very dysfunctional and painful relationships. If you attracted and married a partner who was unable and unwilling to meet your marital needs, you most likely have divorced a partner who is unwilling and unable to meet your divorcing needs.

Ted's Time Bomb

"Susan told me that she would pick up Jimmy by six-fifteen on Sunday. Jimmy's favorite show, SeaQuest, begins at seven, and he wanted to get home to his mom's house in time to watch it there, or stay for dinner and watch it with me. I was pleased with the six-fifteen pickup because I had a date for a concert that started at seven-thirty.

"When I saw the clock strike seven, I hit the roof. Jimmy, who had been packed and ready for nearly an hour, turned on the television and took off his jacket. As SeaQuest began, I started recalling every time Susan had ever been late, beginning well before our wedding and continuing long after our divorce. I just kept thinking how she's inconsiderate, slow, and stupid. I was furious, practically enraged, by the time she rang my buzzer at seven-nineteen.

"I threw open the door, waved the concert tickets in her face, and then ripped them up in front of her. I also spit out some choice four-letters words, called her names, and accused her of every sin I could think of at that moment. She said that she had been stuck in traffic because of an accident on the highway. What do I care? All I knew was that there was no way I could pick up my girlfriend and get to the concert on time.

"As my anger rose, so did Susan's, and she proceeded to engage in some major name-calling as well. Poor Jimmy, who often has a hard time with the transition from my house to Susan's, stormed out of my place, screaming at both of us. Now, in addition to hearing

this terrible fight, he missed his favorite show. I felt ter-
rible about the whole mess."

What's Done Is Still Happening

When you get angry at your ex, only about ten percent of
your anger can be attributed to the current situation. The
other ninety percent comes from your past experiences with
your ex, as well as those with your parents, caregivers, and
other significant people. The present situation has simply triggered your past anger and allowed it to resurface. It's been
said that if you're hysterical, the cause is probably historical.

Also, the longer you and your ex were together, the more
extensive and rich your history. Each partner often knows
precisely which button to push and exactly where to strike to
intentionally hurt the other. In a divorce, the need to strike
back, where it hurts most, is often present.

"I sometimes think Susan comes late just to torment me,
or at least to wreck any plans I may have with my girl-
friend. It makes me so crazy that I want to do something
to get back at her, like leave Jimmy home alone so that
she sees the consequence of her lateness, but I know I
can't do that. I can't do anything that could possibly hurt
Jimmy. I get so aggravated and frustrated and just plain
tired of putting up with her crap."

Renegotiating Your Relationship

Your marriage is over. Unfortunately, when children are involved, that doesn't mean that your relationship with your ex

is over too. For the sake of your children, the marital relationship must now change and develop into a parenting relationship. This change, however, is often difficult.

If it were easy to make the transition from the marital to the parenting relationship (or if it were easy to deal with jerks), there would be no need for this book. But because it's not easy, it helps to look at the things that prevent us from seeing the need to change. Once we see the need, we can then learn the techniques or skills that will enable us to deal more effectively with the jerks in our lives.

Among the things that prevent us from seeing a need to change are highly charged emotions like anger, jealousy, and fear.

Anger

Anger makes us feel stubborn and unwilling to change. When we're angry, we dig in our heels and deliberately do the opposite of what we're being asked, even if what we're being asked is to our ultimate benefit. Instead of clearly seeing what changes we can make to get what we want, we have a tendency to seek revenge at all costs.

It's easy to allow your feelings of rejection, abandonment, and betrayal to turn into anger after your divorce. And it's even easier to allow that anger to cloud your judgment about the need to change.

Jealousy

Jealousy also clouds your judgment. It can cause you to blow things out of proportion, to believe things that aren't true, to disregard things that are obvious, and in general to over-react. While anger sometimes clouds reality, it usually directs your actions. There's nothing directive about jealousy, however. It's like blowing a gray fog over everything.

At times, it's difficult to see through jealousy to the need for change and to see clearly whether the problem you're having with your ex is a real issue or if you're feeling envious in some way.

Jealousy of one's ex is common. Perhaps your ex has gone on to become successful in business while you're having financial problems. Or your ex has a very attractive new partner and you're not seeing anyone. Maybe your ex is having another baby when your biological clock has ticked away. All of these things can stir up jealous feelings in you. It may help to know that it's rarely as great on the other side of the fence as it seems.

"I went into a jealous depression when my ex remarried. I didn't want to let our sons attend his wedding and wouldn't buy them suits. I had fantasies about wrapping his wife's bouquet with poison ivy and spreading salmonella all over the main course at the reception. When a hurricane forced them to cut their honeymoon short, I claimed it was because I had put a voodoo doll of him in the washing machine. We still had some friends in common, and because I was such a pest about the wedding and honeymoon, asking the details and stuff, most of them stopped talking to me. Now it's seven years later and he's divorcing this wife, too. He's got another child, a daughter, who's two, and now he has to pay to support them as well. I heard that he recently moved into a studio apartment. On the other

hand, things have really settled down for me a lot. I was promoted at work and just bought a new house. And our sons, who are now twelve and fourteen, are going away to camp for two months this summer, so I just signed on for a singles share at a beach house. I have a lot of things to look forward to these days. I'd choose my life over his any day."

Fear

Another reason we have trouble changing is because there's a hidden payoff in keeping things the same. Familiar dynamics, even if they are abusive or hurtful, are more comfortable because we know what to expect. On the other hand, changing means risking the unknown. And for most of us, fear of the unknown is stronger than the misery of the present situation. It's the "devil you know is better than the devil you don't know" philosophy.

Of course, the problem is that if you want things to be different, you have to change the way you do things. If you do something the same way over and over, you'll get the same results over and over. If you do something the same way over and over, and expect different results, you'll go nuts. The key to getting different results, therefore, is to change how you do things in the first place. Face your fear of the unknown, look beyond your jealousy and anger, and leap ahead!

Doing Things Differently—Beginning Now

In most divorces your self-esteem takes a big hit, and it often takes all you can do to rebuild it. For many, it means finding a good therapist or a self-help group. For others it may mean starting an exercise or eating plan. In any case, rebuilding self-esteem almost always involves change and doing things differently. While putting off change until tomorrow may be a familiar route, starting now can jump-start your self-esteem and head you in the right direction. Be aware that this book asks *you* to change. Your changes will, in turn, affect your ex's behavior.

The Past Is History

"One of the hardest parts for me was admitting that I had been such a bad judge of character in marrying my ex. How could I have fallen in love with such a jerk?! He's selfish, he doesn't tell the truth, and he runs away from his problems. I would like to think he wasn't this way when we were married, but the truth is I don't see how he could have changed in the short time we've been divorced. I keep going over details in my head, trying to figure out how I was so blind to these characteristics before we married and I had a child with him."

This mother could spend her life trying to figure out whether her ex was a jerk before they married or if he turned into one after they divorced, but why waste her time? Trying to figure out what went wrong is like trying to drive backward to undo a car accident. She could also spend her time berating herself and putting herself down, but again, where is that going to get her?

Self-Destructive Self-Talk

"Then I start thinking that maybe I'm not such a great catch either. After all, why would any man want to get involved with a woman with a two-year-old? Especially one who's so tired all the time. And I feel like I look awful. My house is a mess, and I just want to crawl into a hole with a box of chocolates and pull the hole in with me."

A big esteem-diminishing and self-defeating technique we use to keep ourselves from changing is talking ourselves out of it, telling ourselves that we're not worthy of change.

All people talk to themselves. When you're walking down the street, maybe you think: Gee, I forgot to turn off the coffeepot, or: I have to remember to call that new client when I get back to the office. That's self-talk, and it goes on in our heads much of the day. Self-talk can be productive or unproductive.

Productive self-talk promotes change. We say to ourselves, "I want to remember to get that proposal out at work today" or "I'm not sure I told the baby-sitter what time I was coming back; I'll have to call her." Productive self-talk motivates us and can even work as a check-and-balance system. Self-destructive self-talk, on the other hand, blocks our initiative to change and undermines our belief and confidence in ourselves.

The self-destructive messages we send to ourselves often have a basis in the messages we received during childhood and frequently mimic the voices of our parents. "I am a total idiot. I can't believe I forgot that," for example, may have originated in a childhood scolding: "What are you, an idiot? You should know better than that!" The unfortunate thing about this type of self-talk is that it diminishes your self-esteem. And when self-esteem is low, you're less likely to try new things, make new friends, and, of course, make changes in your life, including changing your relationship with your ex.

If you want your life to change, it's important that you take steps to eliminate this type of self-talk from your thoughts. To do this, you must first recognize that you speak to yourself this way. Next, you must make a conscious effort to override the self-destructive message with a constructive one. Because human beings can think only one thought at a time, self-destructive self-talk can be overridden by memorizing other, more positive thoughts and repeating those thoughts over and over to replace the negative ones.

Below are some typical self-destructive self-talk phrases and suggestions for more positive expressions.

Self-Destructive: "I'm a terrible parent."
Constructive: "I'm a loving, caring, good parent."

Self-Destructive: "I'm not very good at this."
Constructive: "I'm learning to do this better."

Self-Destructive: "I can't cope with this."
Constructive: "I can handle this."

Self-Destructive: "My ex was always better at this than me."
Constructive: "My way is different, and it's just as good."

If you feel the negative thought trying to creep back in, try saying to that voice, "I appreciate your comments on the situation, but I'm going to listen to this other thought right now." When you become proficient at getting rid of your negative inner voices, you will free yourself for the positive alternatives. Seeing these alternatives promotes change.

Are You in Crisis Right Now?

Another component that prevents change is the amount of strain you're under at the moment. There are times of crisis in everybody's life, and if you're undergoing a divorce or other major changes in your life, consider yourself in crisis. You may feel lonely, overwhelmed, and even doomed, and, like anger, jealousy, and fear, these feelings are major obstacles to change.

Crises often seem more manageable and less overwhelming if you can think of them as having a beginning, a middle, and an end. By identifying where you are in the "crisis transition" you can more easily see that eventually the crisis will be over. Ask yourself, "When this is over, what do I want?" Making a list of your postcrisis dreams can focus and encourage you to move forward. Maybe you'd like a bigger apartment, more money, a new job. Listing these things can help you clarify that there is life after crisis (and after divorce) and will help you determine how to move forward and change to achieve your goals.

It may also help if, alongside your list of postcrisis goals, you make a list of things that you're grateful for. This "grateful list" sometimes helps you keep the crisis in perspective, to see that maybe, just maybe, you're not doomed after all. Maybe there is a little light in your life right now, just a little something that you can be grateful for.

When "I Do" Turns into "I Don't Have to Anymore"

We've all heard the statistics. The fact is that divorces happen in about 50 percent of all marriages, and today 33 percent of our nation's households with children are headed by a single parent. Experts predict that 60 percent of all children born today will spend some time in a single-parent home.

When a marriage breaks up, the following months and even years can be turbulent for everyone involved. But the dust does eventually settle as new routines and rituals become the norm. For many, though, the problems of creating a new household, dividing the parental responsibilities, and sharing custody never seem to go away. It's helpful, and hopeful, to note that no problem is too big to be solved if it is viewed in its proper perspective and broken down into addressable issues.

In the next few chapters, we discuss how to break down complex problems into manageable pieces, and how to know what to do and how to do it once you've identified the changes that need to be made. In short, we give you loads of tools for dealing with your ex in typical confrontations that will invite him or her to respond to you in a more positive and productive way.

Identifying the Problem (Other than Your Ex Is a Jerk)

It's Always Something

Buddha said, "Life is suffering." Dr. M. Scott Peck starts his best-selling and internationally acclaimed book *The Road Less Traveled* by saying, "Life is difficult."

Once we truly understand and accept that life is difficult and inherently problematic, it becomes easier. "Because once it is accepted, the fact that life is difficult no longer matters," says Dr. Peck.

Before Dr. Peck leads us any farther, he tells us, "We cannot solve life's problems except by solving them." But first we must acknowledge that there is a problem.

Dealing with Denial

Denial, which comes in many forms, is one way to deal with problems. To paraphrase Charles Schulz, the creator of the comic strip *Peanuts*, there's no problem too big to run away from!

Denial is a common element in divorced parenting. Many times one parent sees a problem very clearly while the other denies that it exists at all. The problem with denial, of course, is that it effectively delays us from finding solutions to our problems. Yet many people cling to denial as if it were a cloak that makes them invisible. Your ex may be one of those people. Even if you were to hire a jet to write "There's a problem here!" across the sky, if your ex is in denial, it's clear that you'll get no help from him in solving that problem. After all, why should your ex want to fix something that he feels isn't broken in the first place? To get around this, you will have to engage in some creative problem-solving techniques in order to get the solution you want.

Before a problem can be solved, it must be correctly identified. Often, problems are so complex that their clarification requires several steps.

Step 1: Identifying Your Feelings

*"When Jenny arrived home from spending the weekend
with her dad, the first thing I noticed was her suitcase.
It was bulging suspiciously. I ripped it open, wondering
what my ex had bought for Jenny this time. Inside was
a complete Swiss mountaineer outfit, made of gray
suede with little pink and blue flowers embroidered on
the child-sized suspenders. I exploded in anger.*

*"I'm embarrassed about this now, but I was so
angry that I went screaming to Jenny, asking her where
this outfit came from. When she answered, 'Daddy
brought it back from his trip,' I really lost it. So that's
where he was last weekend—skiing! I thought to myself.
And he said he was working. What a jerk!*

*"I flung the tiny outfit across the room and was
dumping the rest of the suitcase's contents on the floor
when Jenny came in, asking what was the matter with
me. She looked so sweet when she asked, 'Don't you like
the outfit Daddy brought me from Switzerland?'"*

Jenny's mom, Nancy, knew that her reaction to finding
the gift was out of line, but it wasn't until she calmed down
and thought about it that she realized why she was so upset.
In her eyes, the expensive outfit was a waste of money. Jenny
would never wear it. But more than that was the fact that she
was angry that her ex was able to take a trip to Switzerland.
They had planned to go skiing in Switzerland six years
earlier and then she'd gotten pregnant with Jenny, so they
had postponed the trip. Then came the divorce. Not only was
she jealous that her ex had finally gotten to go, but she was

also so busy at work that she couldn't go away now at all or even in the near future.

Separate the Feelings from the Problems

It's important to separate your feelings from true problems. For example, the problem here isn't that Nancy's ex is a jerk. That's how she *feels* about him. The fact that Nancy doesn't have the time to go to Switzerland is a problem. Jealousy that her ex got to go is a feeling. Feelings become problems only if you *act* on them inappropriately. Fantasizing about seeking revenge on your ex is not a problem. Pelting his car with rotten eggs *is* a problem because you acted on your negative feelings.

Many times problems are not only complex but also charged with intense feelings such as anger and jealousy. This can cause you to feel overwhelmed, as Nancy was, and result in a kind of paralysis that makes you unable to clearly view the various components of a complex issue.

Get to the Bottom of Things

In situations where you experience very intense feelings, it helps to ask yourself what's behind those feelings. Can you isolate an instance in your history, in your marriage, or in your childhood where something like this happened? Are you holding a grudge? Is your ex treating you the way your parents treated you? Are you expecting something from your ex that you really don't think he or she can deliver? Are you frightened that this situation will escalate? Are you feeling helpless?"

Identifying and Claiming Your Feelings

All people experience a large assortment of feelings, yet most have trouble labeling their subtle emotions with the correct feeling word. It's like understanding a language when someone speaks it to you but not knowing which words to use in reply. Most of us have a tendency to generalize our feelings into four main categories: anger, depression, fear, and happiness. We say, "I'm furious at him." "I'm so angry at her, I could kill her." "I'm so depressed." "I'm too scared." "I'm feeling happy today." All of our negative feelings get categorized as anger. Helpless, hopeless, or sad feelings are labeled depression. Anxieties are grouped as fear, and any positive feelings are termed happiness.

These main categories end up masking the true, subtler emotions that underlie them. Take a look at the following list of feeling words:

accepted	bored	conniving
adequate	brilliant	contemptuous
adventurous	calm	content
afraid	caring	contented
amused	cautious	cranky
angry	cheated	crazy
anxious	cheered	creative
apathetic	comfortable	daring
ashamed	competitive	defeated
bashful	concerned	defiant
boastful	confident	delighted
bold	confused	depressed

disappointed	gutsy	mellow
discouraged	happy	miserable
domineering	hateful	nervous
down	helpful	noble
eager	helpless	nonchalant
efficient	hesitant	nostalgic
egotistical	hopeful	overjoyed
elated	hopeless	overwhelmed
embarrassed	humble	pained
encouraged	hurt	passive
energetic	impatient	peaceful
enthusiastic	important	peppy
envious	impressed	playful
excited	infatuated	pleased
expectant	insecure	possessive
fascinated	insignificant	pressured
fiendish	inspired	proud
foolish	irresistible	provoked
forgetful	irritated	pushed
free	jealous	refreshed
frustrated	kind	rejected
full	lazy	relieved
glad	let down	remorseful
gossipy	lonely	resentful
grateful	lovable	satisfied
great	lovely	scheming
greedy	loving	secure
guilty	martyred	shy

skeptical	tender	uneasy
stupid	threatened	unhappy
successful	timid	unloved
sulky	tired	unsure
surprised	tranquil	vulnerable
suspicious	trapped	warm
sympathetic	triumphant	weary
talkative	uncomfortable	wonderful
tempted	understood	worried

As you read through the list, you probably recognized having felt all of the feelings at one time or another. Most people have. Yet very few people take into account the subtle differences in their feelings when they put a name to them. These subtleties are important, however, because when we have trouble differentiating mild irritation from intense anger, or helplessness from depression, we run the risk of blowing challenging situations out of proportion. In addition, we create an inability to break down situations so that they're more manageable and easier to handle.

Practice differentiating between the subtle feelings you have about your ex. It takes time and patience to learn this skill, but it's well worth the results you'll achieve. Try these on for size.

"I'm grateful that I'm not married to that jerk!"

"I'm impatient when my ex is late."

"I was miserable in my marriage."

"I'm overjoyed with my new freedom."

"I'm skeptical about any plans for a reconciliation."

"I no longer feel trapped."

"I'm delighted with the new Mercedes I just won!"

Step 2: Taking Responsibility for Your Feelings

Once you become more skilled at differentiating your feelings, you'll find it easier to take responsibility for them. Taking responsibility means admitting that no one can make you feel a certain way. Your ex doesn't "make you" feel angry, frustrated, or disappointed; you simply feel that way. Another person may not feel angry, frustrated, or disappointed by your ex, even though she may have behaved in the exact same way. Different people can feel differently as a result of the same action.

When you own your feelings, you place yourself in a position of power and control. To do this, we suggest a two-step process:

Examine whether your initial feeling is masking a subtler one. For example, if you're furious because your ex didn't pick up your child on time, and it ruined your plans, is it possible that your anger is masking a feeling of helplessness or frustration?

Once you've decided what you're feeling, put it into words. For example, let's say your anger is masking frustration that you have to change your plans when your ex is late. Instead of saying, "My ex makes me furious," take the subtler emotion (frustration), and say, "I feel frustrated that I had to change my plans." In owning your subtle feelings, you've changed the situation from one where you had no control (because you can't change your ex or your feelings about him) to one that feels slightly more manageable (because you can make alternate arrangements that will ensure that you don't have to change your plans whether your ex is late or not).

The Bigger Picture

Identifying and owning your feelings are really part of a larger technique called the Think-Feel-Do cycle. When you understand how this cycle works, you will be able to make even more changes that ease the tension and frustration of coparenting with a jerk. Here's an explanation using Susan and Ted from the previous chapter.

The Think-Feel-Do Cycle

Most people believe that when an event occurs, you feel a certain way.

For example, Ted might believe that Susan's lateness causes him to feel enraged. He then might feel helpless as well, because he knows he can't change Susan's actions. What Ted doesn't realize, however, is that events do not cause him to feel a certain way. Events trigger thoughts, and the *thoughts* trigger feelings.

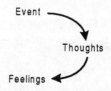

Because the thoughts are so fleeting, people are often unaware of them. Thus, people act solely upon their feelings. When they finally do act, this action causes the next event.

When your thoughts are negative, they trigger negative feelings, and when you act based on those feelings, you usually act in a negative manner, which causes the next event to be negative. On the other hand, when your thoughts are positive, they trigger positive feelings, and the subsequent action is positive. For example, if the phone rings at a time when everything is going well, you optimistically wonder who's calling. You feel curious and excited about the possibility of speaking to a friend or hearing good news. But if you are anticipating bad news, the ring of the phone produces the thought that something's wrong. You feel a sense of dread, worry, and fright.

Your feelings then cause you to act. If you are excited, you run to the phone and eagerly pick it up, and if you're apprehensive, you slowly turn, perhaps pausing anxiously with your hand on the receiver until it rings one more time. When you finally pick up the phone, that action causes the next event in your life.

Here's a diagram of the Think-Feel-Do cycle using Ted and Susan's original scenario.

When you understand that your feelings are triggered by what you think about an event and not by the event itself, you gain a measure of control. Although you cannot change the things (events) that happen to you, or change your feelings (after all, you feel the way you feel), you *can* change your thoughts. A change in thoughts often radically alters your feelings.

Let's start with Ted's thoughts about Susan's tardiness. Some of the thoughts that came to his mind were, "She's always late. I'm going to be late. Jimmy will miss his show. I hate her. She's ruined my life. I wish she would die." These thoughts triggered his anger, and his anger caused him to explode verbally, to act out by throwing open the door and ripping up his concert tickets.

Changing Your Thoughts

In any "Think-Feel-Do" cycle, you are given two windows of opportunity that enable you to make a change in the cycle.

Many times, simply being aware that your thoughts exist is enough to alter your feelings in a cycle. Sometimes, however, it's necessary not only to be conscious but also to actively rehearse alternate thoughts to keep negative ones from affecting your cycle. The more you practice using alternate positive thoughts, the easier it becomes to see the positive side.

Now let's see how it would look if Ted changed his thoughts about that evening through this window of opportunity. His thoughts could have been: Well, better late than never, even though better never late. Maybe I can exchange the tickets for another night. Actually, I'm glad to have a little more time with Jimmy. Maybe she'll be so late that he can watch the show here. I can always hear a concert, but time with Jimmy is precious. You know, I'd love to watch this show with him. Maybe she'll be willing to sit in her car until the show is over." If Ted had these thoughts when he opened the door, things would have been different. He wouldn't have called Susan names and given her ammunition to start the cycle over.

Changing Your Actions

Another window of opportunity that you can take advantage of involves changing what you do, no matter what feelings you have, by utilizing some proven communication techniques and replacing your normal, reactive communication in a cycle with some proactive communication. The remainder of this book is devoted to doing just that.

Step 3: Breaking Down the Problem

Once you have identified your feelings and owned them, looking at the Think-Feel-Do cycle in the process, you're then ready to break down complex issues into their more manageable components. Let's take a look at a complicated problem that Mindy is having with her ex.

"When I found out John was having an affair, I told him he had to move out. He claimed he didn't have enough money for a security deposit on a new apartment, and then I found out, through Timmy, our six-year-old son, that John took his babe to the Bahamas for a long weekend. Well, I got so angry that I threw all his clothes into a pile and left them in the basement of our apartment building. Then, when he finally showed up to get the rest of his things, he told me that he lost his job so he's moving in with his sister. He insisted that Timmy spend the weekends with him, but I can't stand his sister. Or her kids. They're rude, crude, and mean to Timmy at times. I finally gave in and said that Timmy could go for a weekend. And you know what my

ex did? He told Timmy that if Mommy didn't let Daddy move back in, he'd have to move away and never see him again. Can you imagine how upset Timmy was? He came to me in tears! What am I going to do with this jerk? And when I attempt to talk to John, he just shrugs his shoulders and walks away. He thinks everything is fine, that I'm being unreasonable."

At first glance, Mindy's problem seems huge and unmanageable. One of the reasons it seems so challenging, however, is that it is not one, but many problems. Mindy is feeling overwhelmed by a challenging situation. As many of us do when we feel overwhelmed, she has lumped many small problems together to create one huge one that feels insurmountable. If you look closely, however, you'll see that the example above reflects more than eleven problems. (1) John had an affair. (2) John needs to find an apartment. (3) He doesn't have enough money for a security deposit. (4) John acts irresponsibly by taking off to the Bahamas. (5) John confides about his new girlfriend to Timmy. (6) Mindy acts immaturely by throwing out John's clothes. (7) John has lost his job. (8) John is moving in with his sister, whom Mindy can't stand. (9) John tells Timmy that he might have to move away and will never see him again, placing blame on Mindy. (10) Timmy is afraid he'll never see his dad again. (11) John denies responsibility for the problems.

What Exactly Is the Problem Here?

Mindy, whose husband has just flown off to the Bahamas, has many different feelings right now. She has her choice of which feelings to deal with first. To start off, she's enraged about John's infidelity. And hurt. She's also sad about the end of her marriage and afraid of what the future will bring. And she's insulted about being lied to about the money. She's frustrated that John won't talk about or admit to the problems that exist. And she's uncomfortable that he confided about his new girlfriend to Timmy. She's also jealous that she doesn't have a hot new lover.

To Solve or Not to Solve

Before you set out to solve any problem, whether or not it involves your ex, you most likely ask yourself two questions: "What exactly is the problem?" and "Is it worth my time and energy to solve it?" To answer the first question, isolate the problem by looking at your Think-Feel-Do cycle and determine which feeling or feelings are the most intense and then look at which thoughts are causing those feelings. Then, after you have gone through this process, ask yourself if it's worth your time and energy to solve it.

Isolating the Problem

Let's look at how Mindy answers these questions. She wants to get her life back on track but is so upset with her ex that she doesn't know what to do next.

1. **What feeling or feelings are the most intense?** Mindy must first decide which of her feelings is the strongest. Since this may change from day to day or even from moment to moment, she should start with the most intense feeling. For example, she may be more worried about her financial situation tomorrow than she is today. Yesterday, she may have been furious that John took his babe to the Bahamas. Today she realizes that

her concern about Timmy going to his aunt's house is steadily nagging at her and could be described as the most intense.

2. **What are the thoughts causing that feeling?** Upon reflection, Mindy recognizes these thoughts: I can't stand John's sister. She always takes his side. Her children are rude and mean. I don't want Timmy to have his feelings hurt. I hate it that he's putting Timmy in this situation.

3. **Is it worth investing your time and energy to solve it?** Although John has moved in with his sister, it is probably a temporary situation. Mindy can ask herself if she intercedes at this point, will it prevent the development of a bigger problem? On the other hand, if she chooses to let it go, will the problem go away by itself? She can put her foot down and refuse to let Timmy go, or decide that in a few weeks the circumstances will probably be different.

After a thorough examination of her feelings in relationship to both our questions and the Think-Feel-Do cycle, Mindy decided to let John take Timmy to his sister's house for the weekend. When she asked Timmy about it later, he reported that his weekend was "okay."

Accepting Tolerable Situations

The last question, "Is it worth your time and energy to solve it?" is the most important. Many conflicts between you and your ex are fueled by anger, jealousy, and control, and if you can take a deep breath and "don't sweat the small stuff," you will again move forward on your own life's path.

The serenity prayer, written by Reinhold Niebuhr and widely adopted and used by members of twelve-step recovery programs, asks for the wisdom to know the difference between what you can change and what you can't. Maybe it will be helpful to you: "Grant me the serenity to accept the things I cannot change, the courage to change the things I can, and the wisdom to know the difference."

Acceptance doesn't happen overnight. It's gradual. If you continue to expend your energy trying to change things that don't really matter in the long run, you'll wind up exhausted and frustrated, with no positive results to show for your effort. While we spend the remainder of this book showing you how to change certain situations, it's important that you develop a certain level of acceptance about the things you cannot change.

There is no doubt that raising a child with an uncooperative ex is a difficult task. By accepting that it is difficult, you make it easier. Knowing which problems aren't worth your while to solve frees you to move on, to have more fun, to feel better in general. And when you're feeling better, you can come up with more creative ways to solve the problems that do need your attention and effort. An attitude of acceptance when a problem can't be solved makes room in your mind and heart for solutions to the problems that do need to be solved.

Who Tops the Problem Pyramid

Responsibility

In order to take responsibility for solving a problem, we must first recognize what responsibility means. It means knowing that the choices we make in our lives have consequences and being willing to accept that what happens to us is a direct result of those choices. Taking responsibility gives us power and control, because when we recognize the relationship between our choices and their consequences, then the next time we don't like a consequence, we can make a different choice.

Many times we become bogged down in the problem-solving process because we come up with so many excuses for not solving the problem at all. Yet when you take responsibility—when you, in effect, say, "I will take action, I will do something about this situation," rather than saying, "Something should be done" or "Gee, I can't help it, I can't make a difference here"—you take the first step, which makes you more powerful and puts you in control.

Try the following exercise. Make a list of four or five things you can't do. For example, maybe you can't cook, speak a foreign language, or roller-skate. Say them slowly out loud: "I *can't* cook. I *can't* speak a foreign language. I *can't* roller-skate." See how you feel as you say them.

Now try it a different way. Instead of saying "can't," say "won't": "I *won't* cook. I *won't* speak a foreign language. I *won't* roller-skate." How do you feel now? Most people feel a little uncomfortable. There's more power in the word "won't," and when you say it, you are claiming control and responsibility for not doing those things.

"It's not that I won't *do those things, it's that I just* can't. *I don't have the time. I mean, I'd love to learn a foreign language and to roller-skate, but I've got other priorities."*

Exactly! This person *won't* make those things a priority. He's *chosen* other priorities instead, and that's fine! But he's not a victim of some unseen force and *can't* do them. By saying "won't," however, he can recognize his ability to change his priorities, or his reasons for not changing them. By taking responsibility, he is able to control his decisions better, instead of feeling that he's a victim of circumstances.

Contribute to the Solution

It's important to admit that we sometimes have a tendency to contribute to the problem rather than to the solution. Looking at your piece in the custody puzzle includes examining your own actions, reactions, and motivations for behaving the way you do.

When trying to solve problems with your ex, ask yourself if you are contributing to the problem. One mother admitted to chugging a beer before she called her ex so that she could "get angry" and "be more effective" with him. Although alcohol is socially and legally acceptable from the White House to the Vatican, it is a mood altering-drug, and a depressant, at that.

Sometimes your contribution to the problem involves covering for your ex. One father couldn't figure out why his wife couldn't manage her money and refused to see that he constantly bailed her out of financial holes, which enabled her to remain irresponsible.

Other times, your contribution to the problem involves engaging in avoidance techniques. These enable you to avoid responsibility for coming up with a solution to the problem. At the same time they can allow the problem to continue or get worse. The ones to watch for include justifying your actions, making assumptions, placing blame, projecting the worst, and engaging in deliberate manipulation. Recognizing these behaviors in yourself takes you one more step down the road to having a more peaceful custody relationship. Here are some examples:

Justifying Your Actions

"Our son is having a hard time in school and complains of headaches a lot, especially on Monday mornings. I have always believed that in addition to sick days, we need mental health days. So I don't really have a problem with letting my son stay home if he's upset. Recently, though, the school confronted me about his absences. I told them that he was going through a hard time because of the divorce and it seemed sensible to keep him home. I said that we were doing things that were educational like going to the zoo and watching historical movies I'd rented. I felt perfectly justified until they pointed out that he'd been absent four of the last five Mondays. I guess I didn't realize it had been that many days!"

This mom felt, in her own words, "justified" in keeping her son home from school because he was having a hard time with the divorce and because they were doing "educational" things anyway. But in justifying her actions, she was also successfully avoiding the real issue: Her son was having a hard time with the divorce and was missing a lot of school because of it. Once the school helped her see that she was avoiding responsibility and contributing to the problem by justifying her actions, she was able to get the help for her son that he needed in the first place.

Making Assumptions

"I'm sure the only reason my ex wants to see Nick on Saturdays instead of Sundays in the summer is because she wants to go to an adults-only beach on Sundays."

By assuming that his ex's ulterior motive involves her own selfish pleasure, this father adds an element to the problem that might not be present. For example, would he feel differently if his ex's work schedule had changed and she now had to work on Sundays? When we make assumptions, we contribute to the complexity rather than the simplicity of a problem, making it more difficult to solve.

Deliberately Being Manipulative

"I don't want my ex to go to the hockey awards dinner with us so I'm telling him that we're not going either. Then we'll just change our minds at the last minute and go."

You've heard Sir Walter Scott's "O, what a tangled web we weave, when first we practice to deceive." Being manipulative is dishonest and immature. We often end up having to make up more lies to cover for inconsistencies in our original manipulation. In addition, it sets a terrible example for our children. While it may solve your initial problem, the tangled web that grows from such dishonesty is more trouble than it's worth.

Projecting the Worst

"I just know that whatever toys I send with the kids on the weekends will end up coming back broken or with missing pieces."

Are you a fortune teller? When you project into the future about what "might" or "could" happen, you often end up creatively suffering in the present. Don't add to your problems by projecting problems that haven't even happened yet!

Placing Blame

"Tommy had been having trouble sleeping, and I just knew it was because his father let him watch violent TV shows and movies. When he came home after a weekend there, it would take him three or four days to settle back down and be able to sleep again. I was furious with his father, but what could I do about it? I'm embarrassed to admit it now, but blaming his father was an easy way out. When Tommy's sleeping behavior got worse, I sought professional help, basically so I could have ammunition against his father. The counselor gently suggested that maybe Tommy was having trouble making the transition from his father's house back to his regular routine, and that maybe the shows they

watched weren't the real cause of his sleep problem. When she and I explored that possibility with Tommy together, it turned out that she was right. And we uncovered a whole lot more about the divorce that was bothering him. Once things were out in the open, and we worked on them a bit, Tommy went back to sleeping just fine."

Blaming another person for a problem often keeps you from examining the different possibilities that may underlie the issue. Blame is an effective way of putting on dark shades and looking at a problem from only one point of view.

If you often hear *yourself* saying things like, "I didn't say that," "You didn't tell me that," "You never said that," you may need to take a look at the problem from a different perspective. Draw your Think-Feel-Do cycle. What are *your* feelings, *your* thoughts? What action did *you* take that might have produced a negative event?

We're not suggesting that your ex is blame-free or that he is telling you everything he claims or even that he is remembering everything you have told him. We're suggesting that you *honestly* look at the ways you might be contributing to the problem instead of to the solution. Once you've taken this step, you'll find that the problem becomes much simpler and therefore easier to handle.

Guilt

Another way we subconsciously avoid taking action to solve a problem is by allowing guilt, the "should"s and "shouldn't"s in our lives, to bring us to a standstill. Somehow we believe that if we feel guilty enough, it will absolve us from doing anything about it. A simple grammatical shift, however, can change us from guilty victim to positive achiever and move us forward on the path of effective problem solving.

To make this shift, simply substitute the word "could" for "should" and see the difference it makes in clarifying the choices you have as well as the consequences of those choices. "I should stay inside this weekend and clean out all the stuff my ex didn't take with her when she left" sounds like you have no choice in the matter. "I could stay in this weekend and clean out all the stuff my ex didn't take with her when she left" sounds as if it's one of many choices you could make in deciding how to spend your weekend. "I could make a bonfire with her things. I could invite my friends over to watch me light it. We could toast marshmallows!" There's more power in "could" because it assumes you have options.

Guilt also rears its ugly head because of the perception we have of the way things "should" be. Many times media-fabricated role models (most sitcom Moms and Dads for example) persuade us to believe that we can be supermen and women. Then when we don't *want* to be or do everything, we feel guilty. Likewise, we sometimes believe that we not only *can* do everything, we must also *want* to do everything. When our feelings run counter to this pressure, guilt ensues.

Guilt is helpful only when it keeps us acting in line with our beliefs and morals. Otherwise, it tends to create needless suffering. In addition, because it implies a deep-seated belief that we've done something "wrong," it eats away at our self-esteem and makes it less likely that we will see our future choices and options and be confident about acting on them.

Try switching the word "could" for the word "should" in your vocabulary and see what options and choices it opens up for you. Recognizing these options and claiming responsibility for your choices gives you power. Sometimes that power may scare you, or you may feel a little uncomfortable with it because you're not used to it, but wouldn't it be nice, in situations with your ex, to have power and control?

Claiming Power

It may take some time for you to get used to catching yourself and changing your thoughts, allowing you to take responsibility and empower yourself, so we've provided some common ways many people avoid responsibility, and we've made some suggestions on how to reword those old, powerless choices. By recognizing when you use these (even if at first you don't recognize them until days after you've said them), you'll be on the road to claiming power and taking responsibility for the choices you've made.

Old: "I can't/couldn't [go to dinner, get my career going, etc.] because [my child-care responsibilities are too burdensome]."
New: "I'm choosing not to [go to dinner, get my career going, etc.] because I've chosen to [put my efforts into raising a healthy daughter/son]."

Old: "Why didn't you tell me [Suzy's tuition was due, spring break was coming up, etc.]?"
New: "I didn't [look up the tuition payment schedule, the spring break dates, etc.]."

Old: "You make me [so angry, look bad in front of the other parents]."

New: "I feel [so angry, like I look bad in front of the other parents]."

Old: "If only I didn't have to deal with [my ex, that "jerk"], then I'd be able to get things under control."

New: "It's unfortunate that I have to deal with [my ex, that "jerk"], but I'm working to get things under control."

Old: "I should [clean the house this weekend], but I know I'll never get around to it."

New: "I could [clean the house this weekend], but I may choose to [go to the gym] instead."

Old: "Well, what do you expect from me? I can't help it, I'm going through a difficult time right now."

New: "I'm going through a difficult time right now. I'm trying my best. At least I got nominated for the Pulitzer Prize. Maybe next time I'll win it."

The Flip Side of the Coin— Taking Too Much Responsibility

Once you understand that taking responsibility for your choices gives you control, and you accept that the choices you've made have consequences, you'll be able to make better choices in the future. In addition, learning to phrase your communication without blaming, avoiding, or denying responsibility allows you to begin to identify situations in which you are responsible and distinguish them from the situations in which you aren't responsible.

Because taking responsibility gives you control, there is a temptation to take on too much responsibility. Many people believe that they have to fix everything and everyone, because if they don't, no one else will. These people often take on responsibilities that don't belong to them, such as responsibility for someone else's feelings or problems. The person who takes too much responsibility often feels overwhelmed and unappreciated, while the person who takes too little responsibility feels controlled and suffocated. When this happens, it complicates situations so vastly that it's difficult even to begin working out a solution to the problem.

The Problem Pyramid

People often spend a great deal of time spinning their wheels, trying to solve problems that don't belong to them. For example, when a child feels afraid at night because he thinks there are "monsters" under the bed, many parents set out to solve that problem. They say things like, "Well, let's look under the bed, then you'll see there are no monsters," or they invent a special "monster spray" and go to great lengths to spray the room so the monsters will leave. But do the "monsters" go away? Not likely. The difficulty lies in to whom the problem belongs.

A "monster" under the bed is not the parent's problem; it's the child's. And because the problem belongs to the child, the solution for solving the problem also belongs to the child. We're not suggesting that you abandon a frightened child, but rather that you use supportive techniques that empower your child to come up with a solution himself. (These techniques are described in Chapter Seven, "When Your Child Tops the Problem Pyramid.")

If you fail to recognize that problems like these belong to your child, you will spend a great deal of time, energy, and frustration trying valiantly to help by taking the problem on yourself. Figuring out to whom a problem belongs in a particular situation does not permit you to wash your hands of it, blame someone else, or rush in and save the day, but rather allows you to decide which course of action to take.

The problem pyramid below will help you sort out who really needs to be taking responsibility for solving a particular problem. Once you know who is responsible, you can decide the most effective way to promote a solution. Read the pyramid from bottom to top:

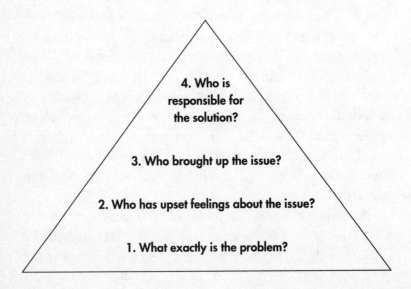

4. Who is responsible for the solution?

3. Who brought up the issue?

2. Who has upset feelings about the issue?

1. What exactly is the problem?

Now let's break it down and discover how this simple formula can enable you to effectively solve a problem like this one: Your ex barges into your home without knocking when she picks up your child.

1. **What exactly is the problem?** By looking at your feelings and identifying your thoughts in the Think-Feel-Do cycle, you can break a big problem down into its individual components and look at them separately.

   Your thoughts in the case of the ex who barges in may be that your ex doesn't live here anymore and has no right to just walk in. You may feel exposed and intruded upon.

2. **Who has upset feelings?** List all parties whose feelings are upset. Note that we don't say all parties who have feelings about the issue. This level is specifically for negative feelings. Because more than one name can go on this level, it's important to look at the next level. If you stop here, you may take on a problem that doesn't really belong to you.

   When your ex barges in, you have upset feelings. Your ex is perfectly content barging in on you.

3. **Who brought up the issue?** Sometimes it is difficult to decide who brought up the issue because it can seem as though two or more people have issues simultaneously. Also, because you're the one who is working through the problem pyramid and who is focused on a solution to the problem, it sometimes seems as though you're always the only one raising an issue. Keep in mind that only one person can bring up an issue at a

time, and it's usually (though not always) the person who verbalized it first.

When your ex is happily barging in, she won't bring this up to you because it's not an issue to her. *You* have an issue with it.

4. **Who is responsible for the solution?** It is the combination of levels 2 and 3 that determines who is responsible for implementing a solution to the problem. If you have upset feelings and you're also bringing the issue up as a problem, then your name will appear on level 4. Conversely, if your ex has upset feelings and has brought up the issue (whether or not she believes it is a problem), then your ex's name belongs on level 4. It is also possible that your child may have upset feelings and be bringing up the issue, and then his or her name will appear on level 4 of the problem pyramid.

It's unlikely that the names on levels 2 and 3 will be different, because people who are content with a situation rarely bring it up as an issue (like the ex who barges in). It is, however, theoretically possible to have different names on these levels. In this case, level 3 alone determines who tops the problem pyramid.

It's important to note that the person whose name appears on level 4 will not necessarily be motivated to find a solution to the problem himself. But *your* next action will be directed by the name that appears here. If your name appears here, you'll use the techniques in Chapter Four, "When You Top the Problem Pyramid." If your ex's name appears here, you'll use the techniques in Chapter Nine, "When Your Ex Tops the Problem Pyramid." And if your child's name appears here, you'll go to Chapter Seven, "When Your Child Tops the Problem Pyramid." (But don't go there now! Keep reading from here!)

Common Problems and Identifying Who Tops Them

To help you identify who tops the problem, look at the following scenarios. We've started you off with fairly simple problems for the sake of clarity and to help you learn the technique more easily.

My ex doesn't pack my son's religion school homework on the weekends I see him.

Who has upset feelings? You

Who raised the issue? You

Who tops the pyramid? You

Daddy makes me go to bed at eight on Saturday nights.

Who has upset feelings? The child

Who raised the issue? The child

Who tops the pyramid? The child

My ex called me at two A.M. because our son was running a 100° fever.

Who has upset feelings? Your ex (and you, for being awakened)

Who raised the issue? Your ex

Who tops the pyramid? Your ex

Now let's take a more complex situation. Let's say that nine-year-old Amy calls her mom, Jane, at seven-thirty on a Saturday night, crying because her dad won't let her watch television and has told her that she must go to bed in a half hour.

> *"I was just about to leave to see a movie when the phone rang. It was Amy, crying hysterically. She was begging to come home because her dad wanted her to go to bed and wouldn't let her watch her favorite TV show. Why does he have to put her to bed so early? Anyway, Amy kept crying and crying. By the time she calmed down, it was too late for my movie. I was angry and exhausted and my night was shot!"*

Now who tops the problem pyramid? At first glance, most people would automatically assume that mom has a problem because she has to miss her movie. In addition, it's clear that Mom has taken sides with Amy. She too feels that the bedtime is ridiculous, and when Mom's feelings are involved and her plans are ruined, she's very likely to assume that this problem is hers and go about solving it. The difficulty is that if Mom decides it's her problem, and takes it up with her ex, tempers are likely to rise and Mom may end up wasting a lot of time and energy spinning her wheels. Let's work through the problem pyramid and see who really needs to solve this problem.

What exactly is the problem? Amy isn't having a good time at her dad's, so she called Mom up crying. Mom's plans to go out are now ruined because she has to spend time calming Amy down.

Who has upset feelings? Amy is upset because bedtime is too early; Mom is upset that her plans are ruined.

Who raised the issue? Amy (If Amy hadn't called Mom, Mom wouldn't have an issue.)

Who tops the pyramid? Amy!!

Because Amy's name appears on the second two levels of the pyramid, the most effective route for Mom to take will involve supporting Amy in solving her own problem. When Mom empowers Amy to deal directly with her dad, she can slip out of the divorce communication triangle and avoid engaging in a battle with her ex over his rules in his house where he has the final authority. By allowing Amy to deal directly with her dad, Amy will feel more confident, more in control and will be less likely to need her mom's help in the future. Subsequently, Jane will achieve her Saturday nights without phone calls from Amy or conflicts with Amy's dad.

In cases where your child has a problem, it's important to remember that even though you're divorced, the bottom line is that you're still a parent, and as such you are responsible for listening to your child whenever he has a problem, even if it affects your plans. We understand that this can be a time-consuming and frustrating process, but if you take the time to empower your child to solve his own problems, it can actually save you time in the future.

Try this one: My ex-wife constantly rearranges visitation whenever our son is even slightly ill. I think her new husband is afraid of getting sick and having to miss work at his "big-shot" job.

Who has upset feelings? The new husband and you

Who brought up the issue? The new husband

Who tops the problem pyramid? The new husband

Now try the next few on your own. Don't get hung up on what the solution will be; simply figure out who tops the pyramid.

1. My daughter is taking antibiotics and my ex never remembers to give her the medicine at the right time.

2. Every few months my ex calls and tells me his whole financial situation, how terrible things are. I'm sure he's trying to get me to reduce what I receive in child support.

3. My ex thinks its perfectly okay for our daughter to skip her softball practice on the weekends she's with him.

4. My ex screams at me about our daughter's grades. I think she's doing fine, considering the stress she's under.

5. I hate Daddy's new wife. She makes me wash the dishes and clean the whole house. I'm never going there again!

6. My ex always gives our son bigger presents than I can afford.

7. Mommy is so mean! She makes me *walk* home from school every day.

When you've figured out who tops the problem pyramid, you'll know who is responsible for implementing the solution to each of these problems. Remember that no matter who tops the problem, you'll still take steps to promote the solution. The pyramid simply directs your actions.

Answers to Who Tops the Problems

1. You **2.** Your ex **3.** You **4.** Your ex **5.** Your child **6.** You **7.** Your child

When You Top
the Problem Pyramid

Pick Your Battles

Just as with many toddlers and teenagers, picking your battles applies to your ex. Before you raise an issue with your ex, think it through carefully and ask yourself if it's really important. While you certainly need to stand up for what you truly believe, sometimes it doesn't really matter if your child wears her mittens, feasts on junk food one day a week, gets that bath tonight or tomorrow night, or even if your ex returns that sweater you just bought for your child before the winter is over. Sometimes, it may be more to your benefit to just take care of things yourself.

> *"Jake spends Tuesday nights with his dad. When I clean out his lunch box on Wednesdays, I find candy wrappers, cookie crumbs, and chips. I don't even think his Dad packs a sandwich, just junk. I want Jake to have a healthier lunch, but I decided it wouldn't really get me anywhere to bring it up with his dad. So now I either drop Jake's lunch off at his school on Wednesdays or I pack him a lunch of fruits, breads, and juice the night before and send it with him."*

Setting Yourself Up for Success

Sometimes you can prevent a problem from occurring by going that extra mile. Other times you can diminish the impact of the problem by intervening. There are also times when it's in your best interests to look the other way. But when you top the problem pyramid, you need to set yourself up for success before you take any kind of action by formulating a plan of action.

Creating a Plan of Action

Have you ever gone on a car trip where you didn't need to be anyplace at a specific time? Or this trip, you could drive until you got tired, see the sights along the way, stop at a motel when it seemed convenient, then continue whenever you woke up the next morning. It's a wonderful way to travel. There's no pressure and no stress. But would you travel this way if you had to make a business meeting? Of course not. It's inefficient and imprecise. You would probably miss the meeting if you didn't sit down ahead of time, plan the number of miles you'd be traveling and the most direct roads to get there.

Like taking a car trip to a business meeting, topping the problem pyramid means that you must drive the car and plan a trip (in this case a communication trip) that will get you where you want to go in the shortest amount of time.

The plan of action is simply the planning of the trip. This should include several pieces of information: When and where you will speak with your ex, what your "out" is, what your "I" message will be, and what consequences you will use if the "I" message isn't heeded.

When and Where to Speak to Your Ex

While the techniques we describe can be used on the spur of the moment (and can be extremely effective if applied this way), it is always better to set up a time and place to speak to your ex. Again, it's like going on a business trip. If you had to drop everything all of a sudden and leave immediately you might forget to pack your underwear. You still might make it to the meeting on time, and handle yourself well, but you'd probably feel uncomfortable with no underwear.

When you make an appointment with your ex to discuss an important issue, you are asking her to give you her undivided attention for a few minutes. It sets the stage for problem solving and clears it of unrelated clutter, like past resentments. It also gives both of you time to think through your positions on the given subject, to prepare your arguments logically, not emotionally, and to feel comfortable and informed.

When you don't arrange a time in advance, you are inviting your ex to discount you and you are catching him off-guard. He may be angry about something totally unrelated to your issue and displace that anger onto you. You may evoke an emotional response rather than a logical one. In many cases, the old adage, timing is everything, is true. Look at what Nancy had to say about an exchange with her ex, Ben. You will see the difference an appointment can make.

> *"I met this guy, Jim, through work, and he asked me out for Friday. I hadn't been on a date in months and I was really excited. Plus, my daughter, Diana, was staying with her father for the weekend. Well, I got home on Friday and there was a message on the machine from Jim saying that something had come up and he couldn't make it. I was devastated—disappointed that I wasn't going out and angry that he hadn't spoken to me in person. In the middle of all this, my ex, Ben, rings the doorbell and the first words out of his mouth are, 'Why does Diana have to go to the dentist twice a year? Isn't once a year enough for a checkup? And did you have to pick the most expensive dentist in this area? There must be someone cheaper.' As he went on and on and on about the dentist, I lost it. I slammed the door in his face. Diana heard us shouting and got all upset. What*

*can I say? I guess I made a mess out of everything—
again."*

Ben made the mistake of trying to discuss an important
matter without making an appointment. If he had called
ahead of time and said, "Listen, I really need to talk to you
about Diana's dental bills. Is this a good time?" Nancy could
have said, "No, it isn't. I'm wrapped up with work right now.
How about tomorrow morning around ten?" or "Sure, now is
as good a time as any." When making an appointment with
your ex, no matter which of you brought up the issue, it's
always a good idea to set a time within the next forty-eight
hours and be prompt about keeping that appointment.

Find a Neutral Territory

Once you have made an appointment, you need a place to
meet. It's best to choose a neutral setting—someplace
outside of either of your offices or homes. This ensures that
the children aren't running around or listening in. Leave
plenty of time so you don't feel pressured by outside responsibilities.

> *"Martha called and said she wanted to talk about the
> visitation arrangements. I told her that I couldn't talk
> now but that tonight would be good. She said fine and
> then suggested we meet at her place. When she men-
> tioned her place, which used to be 'our' place, I felt the
> hairs on my neck stand up."*

Meeting on your ex's territory puts you at a disadvantage, especially if it used to be your home too. Being there

may distract you. You might find yourself looking around to see what has changed and what hasn't. In addition, it's typical for old surroundings to trigger old patterns of behavior and dynamics between you. Likewise, going to your ex's office could place you in an unbalanced position. For example, it's common to see someone sitting behind a desk as being in a position of authority. If your ex assumes that position, your argument or issue may be substantially weakened because your feelings of discomfort could affect your level of confidence.

If you can't discuss something on the phone, go to a coffee shop, a museum, a department store, or a park bench.

Reframe Your Relationship— This Isn't War, It's Business

Old patterns of behavior are difficult to break. Before you go into a meeting with your ex, it's helpful to look at your relationship with him or her as a business, not a personal relationship. Consider your children your most valuable assets and your ex as a business partner or client with whom you must work in order to keep those assets intact. As you go into your meeting, ask yourself if this were a client to whom you were trying to sell something, or if he had a million-dollar account that you wanted to secure, how would you handle things? How would you handle a client who misunderstands and resists you? Most businesspeople don't engage in a verbally abusive war with each other. A resistant client is treated with kid gloves, especially if he has an account you want.

Keep your feelings out of the negotiating process with your ex. You wouldn't share that you're feeling fat, ugly, and depressed with a client, nor would you tell her that you've just met the love of your life and you've never been happier. Keep your focus on your assets (your children) and the business at hand.

As you would with a client, actively watch for opportunities where you can admit that your ex has a good idea. This is known as win/win negotiating. In business, it helps clients feel important and listened to. While it may be more difficult to do with your ex, it will have the same effect.

> *"My ex called up with a suggestion for the holidays. I've realized that I'm prejudiced about everything he says these days. So I initiated this experiment. I pretended that it was Mel Gibson calling with the same suggestion. And you know what? It didn't sound so stupid coming from Mel."*

Finally, as in any good business relationship, be honest and prepared to deliver what you promise. If you know you can't be flexible on Sunday, don't say that you can. If you know that you're going to let Seth go on that overnight birthday party, don't lie and tell your ex that you're not.

What Do You Want from Your Ex (Besides a Death Certificate)?

Knowing what you want from your ex before you start your meeting, just as you would in business, will keep you focused and will usually get you the results you want.

"My ex's checks kept bouncing and my bank was on my case about it. My ex claimed that it was his bank's fault. I decided before our meeting that I wanted a letter of apology from his bank to my bank, and my ex said, 'fine.' I was amazed."

The Formula

When you top the problem pyramid and have a situation that you would like to change, we recommend that you use an "I" message in speaking to your ex. "I" messages are concise verbal statements that target a specific action, relay your feelings, give one reason why you feel that way, and request a change in behavior. They are a powerful communication tool that will work not only on your ex-spouse but also on your kids, your parents, your boss, your employees—virtually anyone!

"I" messages come in several different forms, starting with the simplest statement of how you feel: "I feel angry." Some people suggest a two-fold message, one with the feeling, and one with the change: "I feel angry. Please try to be on time."

The "I" message we recommend was first suggested by Michael Popkin in his Active Parenting workshop and book. It has four distinct parts, and we consider it more complete than other "I" message forms you may have read about. The four parts are: (1) identifying the problem; (2) stating how you feel; (3) stating why you feel that way; and (4) making a specific request for change.

1. When you _____
2. I feel _____
3. Because _____
4. I would like you to _____

Here's what it sounds like:

When you are late picking up Michael,

I feel frustrated

Because it makes me late for my evening plans.

I would like you to please pick him up on time.

"I" messages are powerful and effective because it takes a moment and some thought to formulate them. This means that you have a moment to get control of yourself, and you'll be concise when you do speak. In addition, they give you ownership, not only of your feelings but also of the problem, which empowers you. They also allow you to give the other person the most information in the shortest period of time. The "I" message may seem like a lot to remember, but because there's a simple formula that you can memorize, it prompts you to continue until your communication is complete.

Positive Action Statements Disarm Your Opponent

When you word the last statement of the "I" message in a positive way, such as, "please watch your language" rather than "please don't swear," or "please be on time" rather than "please don't be late," you create a positive expectation for the other person. When you phrase things negatively— "don't do this," "stop doing that"—you essentially send the message to the other person that you expect him to do the "wrong" thing. You also are criticizing him, which probably will make him defensive. People often fail to hear the words "don't" and "stop" in a sentence, and hear only what follows. If you say "Don't swear at me," what they hear is "Swear at me." Or they tune out and fail to hear anything after "don't."

By giving the other person a request for positive action (something that she *can* do), you disarm her. When you say "please watch your language in my presence," she hears exactly what you said. It becomes a positive, rather than a negative expectation, and all people (even jerks) are likely to live up to our expectations, positive as well as negative.

"I" Messages Address Both Genders

Much has been written about the differences in the communication styles of the genders. John Gray's *Men are from Mars, Women Are from Venus* and Deborah Tannen's *You Just Don't Understand* provide good examples of how difficult intergender communication can be. We're not saying the *y* chromosome has either damaged or enlightened one special side of the brain, arguing nature versus nurture, or playing on stereotypes, we're just making the point that most men communicate differently from most women.

One of the best things about the "I" message is that it addressed both genders' communication preferences equally. Women have a tendency to be tuned into and sensitive to feelings. They respond well when another person talks about how he feels. Men, on the other hand, prefer to know where they stand. They don't want all this "emoting" going on. They don't want to know how you feel. They just want to know what you expect them to do about it.

The "I" message covers both. When a man uses it, it reminds him to include his feelings—thus his jerk of an ex-wife is more likely to hear what he has to say, because she likes hearing and talking about feelings. Likewise, when a woman uses it, it reminds her to be specific about what she'd like her jerk of an ex-husband to do about the situation, which is usually all he wants to know anyway.

Because men and women communicate differently, it's extremely important to note that when women use the "I" message, they have a tendency to leave out what they want the other person to do (the fourth part of the message), and when men use the "I" message, they have a tendency to leave out how they feel (the second part of the message). Remember, all four parts are critical to the effectiveness of the message. They cut through the gender differences and make it easier for you to relate to the other person and for him or her to relate to you. Knowing that you might be likely to leave out a part will make you more vigilant when you use your "I" message.

The basic "I" message can be adjusted to be more effective depending on which gender you're speaking to. When you formulate an "I" message for a man, tell him what you would like him to *do* first. "*I would like you to* use more respectful language in my presence. *When you* swear at me, *I feel* angry *because* it is degrading."

When you formulate the message for a woman, tell her what you feel first. "*I feel* angry *when you* swear at me *because* it is degrading. *I would like you to* please use more respectful language in my presence."

Why "I" Messages Work

"I" messages are difficult to respond to in a defensive way. When people feel that they are being attacked or threatened in some way, they become defensive and start protecting themselves. "I" messages don't attack the person; they attack the behavior. They are nonthreatening and inherently respectful, if you keep your tone of voice neutral. We all are much more likely to respond favorably when we don't feel that we have to protect our self-esteem.

Another reason "I" messages work so well is that they allow you to remain calm. By memorizing the formula, much like an actor memorizes lines, you relieve yourself of the pressure to improvise. You do have to come up with the words that go in the blanks, but the formula assures that you will be presenting all of the information in a concise and positive way. Calm, concise people are far more effective and resourceful than raging lunatics!

Even though these new expressions don't come naturally for most, if at least one person uses these techniques in an exchange, explosions are often avoided. And with practice, these communication styles become part of your speech patterns.

Never Use "Always" and "Never"

When using an "I" message, it's important to keep the words "always" and "never" out of it. Things are rarely always or never true, and saying they are invariably inflames the listener. It's important to deal with each situation as if it were excluded from all others, keeping it in the present by not dredging up the past. Granted, half of our anger and frustration occurs from repeated offenses, but if you can focus on what's happening right now, you'll more likely be able to affect a change.

Compare these two messages:

You're always late and you've made me late again. You never consider my schedule. You never budget your time. Why are you always so inconsiderate?

When you're late, I feel angry because it inconveniences me. I'd like you to start out earlier next week so you can arrive on time.

There's a big difference when you send an "I" message, keeping it in the present by removing "always" and "never" and criticizing the act, not the person. When confronted with the second statement, a person is less likely to feel the need to defend herself and is more likely to respond positively.

Making Your "I" Messages Optimally Effective

When you begin using "I" messages, you may have a tendency simply to take your "old" style of communication and fit it into the form. For example, "When you forget to bring Susie's umbrella, I feel furious because you're such an idiot.

I'd like you to use your brain next time." While this may work, it's likely to cause your ex to react defensively to the insult (you're an idiot).

To make it more concise, and therefore more effective, it's helpful to look behind the strong, harsh feeling of fury and determine whether that feeling is masking one of the subtler emotions we talked about in Chapter Two. When an "I" message is based on the underlying instead of the masking emotion, it comes closer to conveying our true thoughts.

Let's take a look at some typical communication and define the masking emotion on which we're most likely to act. Then we'll determine the possible underlying emotion and formulate our "I" message based on that.

Old: "You're an idiot for forgetting Susie's umbrella. Don't you ever think before you act?"
Masking emotion: Anger
Underlying emotion: Worry that Susie will get wet
New: "I feel worried for Susie's health when she gets wet from the rain. I would like you to bring her umbrella next time it's raining."

Old: "Well, you finally remembered Mark's birthday. It must've taken a lot of brain power."
Masking emotion: Anger (communicated with sarcasm)
Underlying emotion: Relief that Mark's feelings weren't hurt
New: "I'm pleased that you remembered Mark's birthday. He is too."

Old: "I can't believe you didn't come to Sarah's school play. You are so inconsiderate."
Masking emotion: Disgust
Underlying emotion: Disappointment

New: "I'm disappointed that you missed Sarah's play. She's having a piano recital next week and I'd like you to come to that."

Old: "I'm not bringing Lizzy over to your house, you jerk. Why can't you get off your butt for a change and come get her?"
Masking emotion: Anger
Underlying emotion: Frustration
New: "When you expect me to drop Lizzy off, I feel frustrated because it inconveniences me. I'd like to work out a schedule so that the responsibility is divided evenly."

It's interesting to note that the most common masking emotion is anger. This information can be helpful to you. Each time you feel angry, try assuming that it's masking something else and stop yourself from saying anything until you have a more descriptive feeling word to use.

Practice Makes Perfect

Start practicing "I" messages today. Try them on your children.

"When you leave your clothes on the bathroom floor, I feel annoyed, because I can't open the door without running over your blue jeans. Please put them in the laundry basket if they're dirty."

Next try your friend:

"When you call me up to complain about how badly your boyfriend treats you, I feel sad because I'm not dating anyone right now. Let's talk about our plans to get together this weekend."

Now try some on your ex:

"When you send Jen to my house without her hat and gloves, I feel frustrated because she needs them. Please remember to pack them, even if it's not that cold out when she leaves your house."

"When you wait until Saturday morning to call to say what time you'll pick up Hannah, I feel inconvenienced because I can't plan my weekend until after your call. I would like you to pick her up by eleven every Saturday morning."

"When you have a party at your house for your other kids and don't invite our son, I feel concerned because I think that his feelings will be hurt when he finds out. Please invite him next time."

Now try one in a different gender form. And be conscious to use feelings other than anger. Speaking to an ex-husband:

"I would like you to send me the schedule for Matt's hockey games. I feel annoyed when you wait until the night before a game and then expect me to change my plans immediately."

Speaking to an ex-wife:

"I feel concerned when you say how much you hate me in front of our daughter, because you are involving her in our conflict. I'd like you to address me privately about it when you're feeling angry with me."

When the "I" Message Meets Resistance

While "I" messages are helpful and powerful, they don't always engender the response that you'd like. "I" messages and taking ownership of a problem often meet resistance because they go against a long-standing chain of command that was consciously or subconsciously set up in a marriage. Even though the marriage is over, it can be very frightening and difficult to change this dynamic. So even if you give the most well-formulated, concise, nonthreatening "I" message that ever came out of anyone's mouth, your ex may have a surprising, or even shocking, response.

When Your Ex Responds by Putting Up a Brick Wall

Sometimes you'll give an "I" message and come up against a brick wall. Your ex doesn't rant and rave, it just seems as though he or she doesn't "get it." In this case, you might want to try rephrasing your "I" message to include a metaphor, a little story that paints a picture similar to the one at hand. Metaphors have a way of depersonalizing an issue and presenting it in a clear, nonthreatening way that can penetrate even the thickest skin. Instead of saying, "You never listen to anything I say," rephrase your thought in an arena that is familiar to the person to whom you're talking. If your ex likes basketball, liken your comment to the game.

> *"When we discuss Tommy's failing grades and you keep answering your other phone while we're talking, it's as if you're the coach of a basketball team and one of your players keeps shooting baskets while you talk. How is that player going to contribute to the team effort when he won't give his attention to the team meeting? I would really appreciate it if you would give me your full attention while we're talking."*

It's important to keep your metaphors short and to include what you want your ex to do differently. Remember that the metaphor is not a substitute for an "I" message; it's a different presentation of it when your ex didn't get it the first time.

When Your Ex Doesn't Give a @#$% How You Feel

Other times, an ex may be so entrenched in his or her old style of responding that he'll rant and rave no matter what you say. If your ex responds to your new communication skill with, "I don't give a @#$% how you feel," then knowing what you want ahead of time and using a nonthreatening, nondefensive statement will help combat this. For example, you might say: "I understand that. I can hear it in your voice." Then repeat what you want. "I'd like you to . . ." If your ex continues to be abusive, disengage immediately to give both of you some time to cool off.

Get In and Get Out

Disengaging during a conversation with your ex requires that you have a plan ahead of time for getting out. Otherwise, you'll wind up using the "I have to wash my hair now" routine, which is too old and tired to be of help.

At the start of the conversation, whether it's in person or on the phone, inform your ex that you have a limited amount of time. There's no need to be specific, but you can simply say, "I have a few other commitments today, so this will have to be brief." Then, if your ex is being abusive, you can say, "We'll have to continue this another time, because I have to . . ." Memorize your "out" or excuse ahead of time so you don't fumble for words when you're in the situation. Again, you want to present yourself as efficient, calm, and collected, even if you're shaking in your boots! Here are a few suggestions:

"I have to go. Someone's at the door."

"I have to go. I have an appointment with my accountant (doctor, hairdresser, dentist)."

"I have to go. I'm meeting a friend."

"I have to go. I promised a friend that I'd pick up her child."

"I have to go. I have to get a letter in the mail."

"I need to pick up the dry cleaning before it closes. We'll have to end in a few minutes."

"I have to go. The Publisher's Clearing House is here to award me that ten million dollars."

Once you give your excuse to disengage, pull out your appointment book and schedule another time to talk. By scheduling another time right away, your ex won't assume you're avoiding him or her, and you will remain in the position of power. In other words, it won't look as though you're turning tail and running, even if you are.

Disengaging during a conversation with your ex will give you the opportunity to collect yourself as well as set up a very important part of the problem-solving process—consequences.

The Consequences:
Setting Clear Limits by Giving Choices

In life, people learn best when they experience a direct relationship between the choices they make and what happens to them because of those choices. As we explained earlier when we talked about responsibility, every action you take has consequences. If you touch a hot stove, you learn not to do that again because you've experienced a direct (and probably painful) consequence to your actions.

When people divorce, the relationship suddenly requires a whole new set of rules. The more of these rules that are spelled out, the better. These rules include setting limits on your ex's behavior, stating what will happen if the limit isn't adhered to (the consequence), and enforcing the consequence. When you top the problem pyramid, it's generally because there is a boundary you'd like respected or a rule you'd like followed, and your ex isn't complying in some way. Basically, the "I" message states the new rules to your ex in a clear, direct way. But when the "I" message doesn't work, you have to set up some consequences to make your point more clearly.

For example, if your ex is constantly late picking up your child, and it's affecting your plans, you must have an idea of what action you can take the next time your ex is late. This action provides the consequences for your ex's late behavior.

Consequences need to be firm and impersonal, not punitive or disrespectful. They should be directly linked to the problem. The idea is not for you to get revenge on your ex, but to come up with something that will work for you as well as encourage your ex to acknowledge and respect the boundary the next time. For example, if you have a hairdresser's appointment at ten and your ex misses the nine-thirty pickup, when he shows up at ten-fifteen, he will find that you are gone, with your child, to the hairdresser's.

Choices

The most effective limit setting includes a choice. (Yes, this is the same principle that you may have used on your toddler.) "Either _____, or _____" is an effective way to phrase a choice. "Either arrive on time, or I'll drop our daughter off at your sister's house and you can pick her up there."

Choices focus the listener on her options in a particular situation. Because there is a choice, your ex will feel as though he has some control over the situation. When a person feels as though he has control, he's less likely to resist or break the limit. On the other hand, if you were to threaten him with, "You'd better get here on time, or I'm going to take our daughter to your sister's house and you can just pick her up there," it's not likely that your ex will arrive on time in the future.

Mean What You Say

When you offer a choice to your ex, it's important to be sure that *you're* comfortable with it. If your ex's sister won't be home, for example, or you're concerned that your daughter will be upset about being dropped off there, you don't want to offer this as a choice. Otherwise, you'll be caught in the position of not being able to follow through with what you said. The next time that your ex is late, he'll know that your choices are really empty threats, and he won't take you seriously. This weakens your position and will make your ex more resistant to other limits you're trying to enforce.

Brainstorming

Many people feel that coming up with creative choices or consequences is the most difficult part of this technique, but in reality, everybody has the capability to problem solve creatively. Like other things, this skill grows easier with practice.

A helpful technique to set the gears of creativity in motion and to increase your repertoire of useful consequences is to brainstorm about what consequences or choices to give your ex. To do this, start with the assumption that no idea is stupid. The goal of brainstorming is to throw every solution you can think of on the proverbial table, including the unrealistic and outrageous ones. Sometimes "crazy" ideas lead to the solution that you've been looking for.

You can brainstorm in any shape and form, but for now, use a paper and colorful pen, preferably a felt-tip or one with ink that flows freely. Write your problem in its simplest form across the top. Then write anything that comes to mind. Write across the paper, write down the sides, doodle. Take a break for a few minutes. During this time relax, breathe, stretch, turn on the radio and listen to the words of a song you like and try to clear your mind. Then go back and weed out some of the more unrealistic or unfeasible ideas. It can take minutes or days to come up with a creative solution. It takes as much time as it takes. If you have a creative friend, ask him or her to help with your process.

Take a look at a few of the consequences that we brainstormed for a consistently late ex and see what other choices you might be able to offer.

> You could go out anyway and leave your child home alone to greet your ex.

> You could take your child with you so your ex arrives to find an empty house.

> You could find a baby-sitter who'll come over on the spur of the moment and charge the baby-sitter's fee to your ex.

> You could run off to the Bahamas and ignore the problem.

This process can go on and on. The point is to shift gears from the "poor me, what am I going to do" to the "I wonder if this would work" attitude. Many of the solutions you come up with may be unfeasible, like leaving your child alone or running off to the Bahamas (though you'd probably really like to!). But once you give yourself permission to brainstorm all the possibilities, you can then choose your best ideas and put them in either/or form. Let's see how the list we brainstormed might sound:

> "Either arrive on time, or I'll leave our daughter to let you in and lock things up when you leave."

> "Either arrive on time, or we won't be there when you do arrive."

> "Either arrive on time, or I'll arrange for a baby-sitter to watch our daughter until you get there, and you can pay the sitter when you pick our daughter up."

"Either arrive on time, or you can pick up our daughter at your sister's house."

"Either arrive on time, or I'm running off to the Bahamas and charging the trip to you!"

Putting your ideas in the form of either/or choices will help you further weed out any unfeasible, unrealistic, or punitive actions. As you can see from the list above, the consequences that are least likely to work really stand out when they're offered in choice form. (At least we hope they do. But in case they don't, leaving your daughter alone is probably unfeasible; not being there when your ex arrives could be construed as punitive; and running off to the Bahamas is probably unrealistic.)

Avoiding All-or-Nothing Traps

Sometimes we get stuck in the brainstorming process because we have trouble seeing shades of gray. Very often we'll see a situation as all or nothing, black or white, when there are actually many different choices available. For example, if you're crossing the street, and the sign says "don't walk," you may think that you don't have a choice. You have to stand where you are until the light changes. But, in truth, you could cross the street against the light (and chance getting hit by a car), but this choice is so obvious that you may not think of it as a choice. Another possibility would be to walk down the street to another corner (which may take you out of your way) and cross when the light changes there. Or you could just go home and forget about crossing the street. Remember that even if you don't like some of the choices, or if they're not feasible to implement, those choices still exist.

> *"My ex walked out on me for another woman, and I was shattered. All I had wanted was a nice home, which we had, and a baby, which we also had. I felt like the rug had been pulled out from under me, and I wanted to die. I was working on the twenty-first floor of a tall office building and I used to spend my time staring out the window, wondering if the pain of landing would be as bad as the pain I was going through.*
>
> *"I mentioned this to a counselor I was seeing and said that I would jump in a minute if not for the fact that my ex and his new girlfriend would then get to raise our child. The counselor took what I consider today to be a big risk and said, 'So take the baby with you.' I was taken aback by his response, and he repeated himself. 'So jump with your baby. You have that choice.' Luckily, it snapped me out of it. While I didn't like the choice he presented me with, I saw that there were other ways to get through the pain I was in."*

Taking It Slowly

Sometimes, no matter how good your "I" message is, and no matter how well and fairly you phrased your choices, you still meet with resistance. Put yourself back in that business meeting when this happens. When a good businessperson is faced with a resistant client, one of the first things that comes to mind is: This is going to take some time. I'll need to take it slowly. He isn't sold on this yet. I don't want to blow it, there's a lot of money involved. Conversely, when you are faced with a resistant ex spouse, your first thought is usually, Here we go again. If I don't get my point across *now*, I'll never get it across. There's a lot at stake here, and I'm going to make him see that! See the difference? When faced with resistance, it's important to take things slowly. It takes time to develop your relationship with your ex into a *working* relationship, especially since the relationship didn't work while you were married.

Asking Questions

When your ex is resisting the limit or solution you're proposing, try asking as many questions as you can. Asking questions makes your ex feel as though you're interested in what he or she has to say. It also gives you a wealth of information that you didn't have previously but can now draw on. In addition, asking questions involves your ex in the least threatening way possible. And an ex who is involved in creating the solution is less likely to object to it later on. Try changing what you might normally say when faced with resistance into nonthreatening questions.

Instead of: "I can't believe you don't see my side!"
Ask: "What would you suggest I do in this situation?"

Instead of: "You'd better shape up or I'll be forced to take action!"
Ask: "Tell me more about what *you're* looking for."

Instead of: "We're going to do this *my* way or not at all!"
Ask: "How do you see this working?"

Instead of: "I can't believe what a jerk you are!"
Ask: "How do you think we could work this out?"

Selling Your Ideas through Repetition

Sometimes it is necessary to reinforce the limits that you consider firm by using the assertiveness technique of repetition. The following incident is a good demonstration of the technique, as well as an indication of how powerful it can be.

"I was having lunch in a bistro one day when a woman at the counter caught my attention. I perceived that she was arguing with the management about her bill. As I listened (which I couldn't help, given the volume of the episode!), it became apparent that she had come in with a coupon that entitled her to a free lunch. The coupon had expired, but they had expressed their willingness to honor it anyway. The management, however, considered lunch to be a salad and a sandwich. The woman had ordered soup, a salad, a sandwich, cheesecake, and coffee. The restaurant wanted her to pay for the soup, the cheesecake, and the coffee, which amounted to $20.

"'I'm not paying,' she said. 'I have a coupon for a free lunch, and I had lunch, and it's supposed to be free, and I'm not paying.' Well, the management spent thirty minutes trying to explain to her what they considered lunch. They argued, they explained, they pleaded. And

the woman just kept repeating 'I'm not paying. A free lunch doesn't cost $20. I'm not going to pay.' And do you know what? They let her go!"

This woman was clearly familiar with the technique of repetition and used it to her full advantage! We're not suggesting you try this with an expired coupon, but see how well it worked for Jane, who wanted her ex to pick up their son, James, at six o'clock.

James's father called and said, "Hi, Jane. Listen, I won't be able to get James before seven. I hope you don't mind."

"Actually, I do. He has to be picked up at six because I have plans."

"I just told you I can't be there till seven."

"I know. I have to leave by six, so James has to be picked up by six."

"Come on, aren't you listening? I can't get there before seven, six forty-five at the earliest."

"Yes, I'm listening. I hear that you won't be here before six forty-five at the earliest. And that won't help. James has to be picked up at six. At six o'clock, he has to be picked up."

"Can't you change your plans?"

"I won't change my plans. James has to be picked up at six."

"All right, all right. I'll be there at six."

"Thank you. I'll see you at six."

When your ex is arguing about a limit that you consider firm, repeat your limit over and over in a definite voice. Keeping your tone congenial improves the effectiveness of this technique. Say, "I understand that it's difficult to be here at six. But that's the time James needs to be picked up." When you mean what you say, and repeat yourself over and over, you'll usually get your way.

Role-Play—Doing Your Homework

If you have an ex who is exceedingly difficult, or if you simply have an exceedingly difficult time with your ex, it might be helpful to practice the techniques you've learned on someone else. Preparation through role-play is often a good investment of your time because it helps you change old patterns of behavior in a neutral, friendly environment where you won't feel as though the mistakes you might make will become a matter of life and death.

Enlist the aid of a good friend to play your ex so that you can practice your new skills before trying them in a real-life situation. To do this, project what your ex's objections might be, and tell those objections to a friend. Have her be as mean and nasty as she can be during the exchange to give you the practice you need for the worst-case scenario. (More than likely, your friend will be tougher than your ex.) Open the conversation with your "I" message. If you have a weak point, put it on the table first. It will lose its power that way. And remember to be businesslike, clear, and firm during the conversation. Then turn the tables and have your friend act as you and you play your ex.

Summing It Up

The "I" message will play a big part in your successful communication with your ex. Knowing in advance what you want and what your limits are, as well as what the consequences will be for your ex if he or she breaks those limits, will take you closer and closer to each goal you set for yourself.

Problems That You
Need to Solve

Now that you know what techniques to use when you top the problem pyramid, let's work through some real-life problems we mentioned in Chapter One. We'll walk you through identifying the problem and give you an example of one possible "I" message and choice you might offer in that situation.

My Ex's Sick Behavior

*"Every time my ex breaks up with a man, she goes to
bed for a few days. That leaves our five-year-old daughter virtually unattended. My daughter doesn't get outside to play, she misses birthday parties, and she just
lies around the house watching television because of
this woman's sick behavior."*

Let's analyze this problem from beginning to end by asking
some questions.

How often does your ex break up with a new boyfriend?

*"In the time we've been divorced, which is three years,
she's had three boyfriends, so maybe every eight months."*

Okay, so what is the problem here?

*"A five-year-old child doesn't go out to play or to sched-
uled activities. She watches television instead, for a few
days every six to eight months."*

Who tops the problem pyramid?

Who has upset feelings? You

Who brought up the issue? You

Who is responsible for implementing the solution? You

What is your most intense feeling?

"I feel disgusted."

What thoughts are causing that feeling of disgust?

*"My ex is such an emotional basket case that she can't
even pull herself together to function. She was just like
that in our marriage, too. One little thing would send
her into a tailspin. Like when we moved one time, she*

found it so 'stressful' that she just sat around on the
couch smoking cigarettes while I did all the work."

**So is this issue with your daughter rooted in your history with your
wife, or are you really concerned that your daughter spends a few
days every eight months watching television?**
  "I guess it's really rooted in my past."

So is it worth your time and energy to try to change it?
  "No."

In analyzing the problem, this person discovered that
creating an "I" message and figuring out consequences for
his ex weren't worth the time and effort that it would take.
He discovered, by looking at his feelings and thoughts, that
his daughter wasn't being harmed by spending a few days
watching television. His sense of urgency was really rooted
in the past with his wife.

For the sake of argument, however, let's see what an "I"
message could look like and what consequences he could
have used if this problem hadn't been rooted in the past. Remember that to be the most effective, the "I" message form
changes depending on the gender of the person to whom
you're speaking. Here's an "I" message for this man's ex-
wife:

*"I feel concerned about Sarah because it seems that she
didn't get out this weekend. When you break up with
somebody and feel too lousy to handle Sarah, I'd like
you to call me so I can take her."*

An appropriate choice might be:

"Either take Sarah to her parties anyway, or call me
and I'll take her."

It's important to note that if this man felt that his ex was physically harming his daughter in some way, by not feeding her, hitting her in order to keep her quiet, or other abusive behaviors, he would want to take some sort of legal action.

My Ex Can Do No Wrong

"My son thinks his dad can do no wrong. But my ex lies to us all the time. He says he can't pick up our son on Saturday morning because he has to work. When I call his office to offer to drop Danny off, he's not there. It makes me crazy!"

What is the problem here?
"My ex lies to us, and Danny thinks his dad is God!"

Is the problem that your ex lies, or that your son thinks he's God?
"Both!"

Okay, let's take your ex's lying as a separate issue, then we'll discuss your son's feelings about his dad.

Who tops the problem pyramid when your ex lies?

Who has the upset feelings? You

Who brought up the issue? You

Who is responsible for implementing the solution? You

What is your most intense feeling?
"I feel crazy. And I'm frustrated."

What are your thoughts that are triggering your feelings of craziness and frustration?

"I keep trying to get Danny and his dad to have quality time together. As I said, Danny adores his father. But his dad keeps getting out of the visitation by lying to me. Why should I waste my time and energy getting them together when his dad is such a jerk? That's why I feel so frustrated. And then when Danny thinks his father can do no wrong, and his dad just lied to me, I get crazy!"

So why should you waste your time and energy trying to get them together?

"But doesn't Danny need time with his dad?"

Can you change the lying?

"No."

Can you change how Danny feels about his dad?

"No."

Is this worth your time and energy trying to change what can't be changed?

"I guess not."

Stop calling Danny's dad to try and find a way to get them to see each other. Arrange a playdate for Danny. Go read a good book. Take Danny to a movie. And hear what the message is that your ex is sending you with his behavior—that he doesn't want to see Danny this weekend, period. Know, too, that if your ex is truly this kind of jerk, your son will eventually see that for himself. Marshal your energy and resources so that when that happens you can be supportive and sympathetic for Danny.

In this scenario, the mother's feelings weren't rooted in the past. In working through the preliminaries prior to confronting her ex, she discovered that it wouldn't be effective to do so. As we've said before, many times we spin our wheels trying to solve problems that probably don't have a solution. The natural consequences—that Danny will probably discover for himself that his dad isn't God—will eventually solve that problem for this woman. The lying is annoying, but if she simply hears the underlying message, that Dad doesn't want Danny that weekend, then why he doesn't will matter less.

Changing Plans

"My ex is constantly changing her plans and then expects me to change mine. I'm really tired of it. But what can I do? If my ex cancels visitation at the last minute, I can't leave the kids alone."

What is the problem here?

"My ex is inconveniencing me over and over so I can't make any plans."

Take out the word "can't" and replace it with "won't." (Replacing "can't" with "won't" helps you see that you've made choices here.)

"My ex is inconveniencing me over and over, so I won't make any plans."

Now, what is the problem here?

"I'm being inconvenienced by my ex and I'm not making plans because I hate having to rearrange them at the last minute."

Good, we'll come back to that. Now, who tops the problem pyramid?

Who has the upset feelings? You

Who brought up the issue? You

Who is responsible for implementing the solution? You

What is the most intense feeling?

"I feel inconvenienced and frustrated."

What thoughts are causing that feeling?

"I want to be able to make plans and know that they'll happen the way I planned. That rarely happens because of my ex's last-minute changes."

So is this worth investing your time and energy to change?

"Yes. I'd like to make plans and be able to stick with them."

Now it's time to formulate an "I" message. (Remember to make it gender effective.)

"I feel frustrated when you change your plans at the last minute because it inconveniences me. I would like you to give me forty-eight hours' notice if you need to change your plans."

What if his ex-wife doesn't respond? What if she agrees to the forty-eight hours' notice but doesn't observe it? Then it's time to formulate a choice and consequence.

"Either call me forty-eight hours in advance or I'll hire a baby-sitter and send you the bill."

If you say you're going to send your ex a bill, do so. Type it up and mail it. Don't expect your ex to hand over cash the next time you see him. Allow him time to write you a check when he pays the rest of his bills. If he doesn't pay promptly, send a "past-due" notice thirty days later.

Safety Issues

"My ex thinks it's perfectly safe to leave our ten-year-old daughter alone. He leaves her alone in his apartment, in stores, in the car, everywhere. I just go nuts when I think of the danger involved."

What is the problem here?
"My daughter is being left alone in places I do not think are safe."

Who tops the problem pyramid?

Who has the upset feelings? You

Who brought up the issue? You

Who is responsible for implementing the solution? You

What is your most intense feeling?
"I feel nervous and afraid."

What thoughts are causing that feeling?
"My daughter might get kidnapped, molested, or hurt in some way without an adult to protect her."

So is this worth investing your time and energy to change?
"Yes!"

Let's formulate an "I" message, remembering the appropriate gender form.

"I would like you to stay with Jennifer in public places or take her with you if you leave the apartment. When you leave her alone, I feel afraid that something serious could happen to her, and I don't think she's old enough to handle the types of problems that might arise."

Suppose her ex doesn't respond to this "I" message. What choice could she give? Well, she might try:

"Either remain in close contact with her or sit down with Jennifer and me and we'll brief her on safety procedures together."

Her ex might be so adverse to sitting down together that he'll automatically choose to remain in contact. Or her ex might choose to sit down with them, which would be fine. An open discussion about safety might make all parties concerned, including her ex, more aware of the dangers involved. It's more likely, however, that her ex will take an "I don't give a @#$%" attitude and choose neither. Then she might offer this choice:

"Either sit down with me to talk to Jennifer, or I'll do it myself."

While this may seem at first to be a half-hearted solution, at least she has informed her ex that she's going to talk with Jennifer about safety. Implicit here is that she'll also be discussing her ex without him there, which he may not like. He may then choose to backtrack and pick one of the choices offered previously. If his attitude remains laissez-faire, the next step in any case would be Mom speaking with Jennifer about safety.

Sometimes when you can't motivate your ex to take action, you must do so yourself. Clearly, if Mom feels that his behavior was life-threatening to Jennifer, she should check with her lawyer to see if legal action can be taken. It's important to realize, however, that episodes like this often involve different parenting values. While one thinks it's safe, the other doesn't. No amount of arguing or negotiating will change these values. Sometimes, a consequence will, but at whose risk? Your child's? While you may want to talk to other parents to see how they would handle a situation, you may decide its worth going to court over or you may realize that as your child gets older, this won't be a problem. The choice is always yours. Otherwise, empowering Jennifer, as we discuss in Chapter Eight, "Empowering Your Child," and keeping the lines of communication open, from Chapter Six, is her next best alternative. Note, too, that sometimes a series of choices must be offered, as this woman did.

The Same Beach

"This summer, I planned to take my son to the beach for two weeks in August. My ex-wife found out and took him to the same beach for two weeks in July. By the time August came, my son said he was tired of the beach and wouldn't go with me. I could kill my ex for undermining my plans."

What is the problem here?
"My ex undermined my plans."

Who tops the problem pyramid?

Who has the upset feelings? You

Who brought up the issue? You

Who is responsible for implementing the solution? You

What is the most intense feeling?

"I feel undermined. And disappointed, too, I guess, because I was looking forward to going to the beach with my son."

What thoughts are causing that feeling?

"I wanted to go to the beach with my son. Why does my ex always have to one-up me?"

There are two problems here. One is that you and your son didn't go on the trip that you planned. The other is that you believe your wife planned this as a way of undermining you. If your wife hadn't taken him to the beach, but he still didn't want to go with you, would that have been a problem?

"Yes, I really wanted to take him."

Then let's address that problem. Is this worth investing your time and energy to change?

"Yes."

This is a good sorting through of the issues. The "I" message should be about his son staying home from the beach. You may be surprised to discover, however, that the person to whom he should give the message is his son, not his ex. Although his ex may have contributed to his son not wanting to go, his son made the decision. The father will be more effective in this case if he addresses his son, rather than his ex, about this issue. Let's try it. (By the way, when you give an "I" message to your child, use the "standard" form instead of one of the "gender appropriate" forms. If it doesn't work in the standard form, then try switching it around.)

"Son, when you tell me that you don't want to go to the beach with me, I feel disappointed because I was really

*looking forward to it. I would like to discuss this with
you and see if we can reach a compromise."*

At this point, Dad doesn't need to offer a choice. Rather, he'll
want to utilize the communication tools that we discuss in
Chapter Six, "Learning to Cooperate with Your Ex" and apply
them to his son.

Party Time

*"When the kids go to visit their father for the weekend,
it's party time. He feeds them junk, lets them stay up all
night to watch R-rated movies, and has no regard for
their personal hygiene. Late Sunday night, he returns
them feeling sick, tired, and dirty. I have a terrible time
getting them up for school on Monday."*

What is the problem here?

*"Well, I really object to their father's values. I mean,
can you imagine? He lets them watch these violent
movies! And then they eat all this junk. And who suffers? Me, on Monday morning when they're cranky and
feeling sick."*

There are actually several problems:

Your values are different from your ex's.

You object to your children watching R-rated movies.

They eat junk food when they're there.

You're suffering because you have to deal with them
Monday mornings.

So who tops the problem pyramid?

Who has the upset feelings? You

Who brought up the issue? You

Who is responsible for implementing the solution? You

What is the most intense feeling?

"I feel angry."

What thoughts are causing that feeling?

"I have to suffer on Monday mornings because my ex lets our kids stay up too late and eat junk."

So is it worth your time and energy to change?

"Absolutely, I can't take it anymore!"

What's your "I" message?

"I want you to return the children early on Sunday, bathed and well rested. When they come home exhausted and dirty, I feel upset because it makes getting to school on Monday morning much harder."

Now that you've formulated the "I" message, look at it closely. Sure, you'd like to have the children bathed, but does it really affect Monday morning for you?

"Well, no, I guess not."

So reformulate the "I" message:

"I want you to return the children early on Sunday and make sure they're well rested. When they come home exhausted, I feel upset because it makes getting to school on Monday morning much harder."

This is better. One nice thing about the "I" message is that it makes our communication very logical and concise.

As this woman found out, it didn't make much sense to include one of her gripes (that they were dirty) in the "I" message at this point. When you include all of your issues within the same communication, it overwhelms the other person and he may feel as though you're attacking him. Again, the goal is to get a change in behavior so that your situation is better, not to do battle.

If her ex doesn't respond, she might offer this choice:

"Either return the children early and well rested on Sunday night, or keep them until Monday morning and take them to school."

Now, what about the other problems that the woman was having? What about the differing values, the R-rated movies, the junk food? Well, she could in fact send an "I" message about any of these. It's often easier, however, to begin with a problem from which you are directly suffering, as she did. In addition, it's unlikely that her ex will change his values, or stop the movies or junk food. If she wants to address these in the most effective way, it would be easier to address her children—especially if they're coming home cranky and feeling ill.

Bedtime and Babies

"Not only does my ex put our ten-year-old daughter to bed at seven-thirty on Saturday night with his three- and two-year-olds, I just found out that he locks them in the bedroom to keep the babies from getting out of bed. Isn't that a fire hazard? What if our daughter has to go to the bathroom in the middle of the night? I don't know how I can, in good conscience, let her visit there again."

What is the problem here?

> *"Well, there are two problems. One is that my daughter doesn't like to go to bed at seven-thirty on a Saturday night; the other is that my ex is locking the door of the bedroom, which I think is dangerous."*

Who tops the problem pyramid about the bedtime?

Who has the upset feelings? Your daughter

Who brought up the issue? Your daughter

Who is responsible for implementing the solution? Your daughter

Who tops the problem pyramid for locking your child in the bedroom at night?

Who has the upset feelings? You

Who brought up the issue? Your daughter and you

Who is responsible for implementing the solution? You

What is the most intense feeling?

> *"I feel scared and angry."*

What thoughts are causing that feeling?

> *"My daughter could be seriously hurt or killed if there were a fire and she couldn't get out of the bedroom, and my ex is a stupid jerk for locking the children in."*

So is this worth investing your time and energy to change?

> *"Yes."*

So what's the "I" message?

> *"I want you to keep the children's door unlocked at night when our daughter is there. I'm concerned that if there was a fire, she wouldn't be able to escape."*

And then her choice could be:

"Either keep the door unlocked, or I will need to discuss the sleepover arrangements with my lawyer."

A *Recap*

1. Decide what the problem is in its simplest form. Include only what is directly affecting you.

2. Determine who tops the problem pyramid.

3. Examine your Think-Feel-Do cycle and name the most intense feeling you have.

4. Recognize the thoughts that are causing your feelings.

5. Ask if it's worth your time and energy to change this situation or solve this problem.

6. If yes, formulate an "I" message.

7. Examine your consequences and give a choice.

Learning to Cooperate with Your Ex

Working at Change

Cooperation means working together toward a common goal. Fostering a spirit of cooperation with your ex means laying down your weapons in the war of divorce in order to protect your children. It means that when your ex begins to argue with you, you don't argue back. It means that you stop being reactive and start being proactive. Your kids should be your priority, and although it may kill you to share them with a jerk, it will hurt them irreparably if you continue to do battle.

It's understandable that you may feel bitter, angry, and vengeful toward your ex, but when you deliberately bad-mouth or argue with him in front of the children, it's as if you're saying those things to your kids. The hurt and confusion they feel at those times can be damaging. We know that nobody's perfect. And obviously there will be times when your child overhears you arguing with your ex, sees the expression on your face, or senses your underlying (and many times valid) disgust and anger. You're human. The point is that no matter what your feelings are, your children will be better off if you keep them as your central focus and work diligently at keeping the parenting relationship civil and cooperative.

There are two ways to work at change with your ex. One is by changing your internal state. You sort through your angry and bitter feelings and obtain insights into those feelings that enable you eventually to change them. Once your feelings are different, your actions automatically change. This is often a lengthy process and many times requires the professional assistance of a counselor. Another way to change is by changing your actions first, no matter how you feel. It's akin to administering CPR to someone whose heart has stopped. You can't get inside the person and restart the heart by changing the internal state. Instead, you work from the outside. You place you hands over the person's breast-bone and push down at regular intervals. This external force eventually changes the internal state, and the heart begins beating.

By learning the cooperation skills presented in this chapter, you're essentially administering CPR to the parenting relationship. When you change your actions in an argument with your ex, eventually your internal state will change too. Remember that although it's okay to allow the marital relationship to die, it's not okay for the parenting relationship to die, because if it does, it's your children who will suffer.

The Fight-or-Flight Response

When you find yourself in a stressful situation, your subconscious automatically assesses your physiological response (sweaty palms, fast heartbeat, rapid breathing, shaking hands, cracking voice) in order to determine what kind of signal it should send to your body. Should it tell your body to run from danger? Should it tell your body to prepare defenses and fight? Or should it tell your body that everything's fine, sit down, relax, and have a cup of tea?

The problem with what your subconscious finds is that it's not discriminatory. It can't tell the difference between the rapid breathing that occurs because you are furious that your ex won't take your child to a birthday party and the rapid breathing that happens when you realize you're being pursued by a wild beast. In either case, your subconscious sends the same message: Run, fight, or be eaten!

This panic signal effectively shuts down the part of your brain that handles language and rational thought. Your reactions include clenched fists, gritted teeth, red face, slamming down the phone, crying. In other words, you respond on a purely physiological level. When that happens, you become unresourceful and ineffective, and you give away your power and control over the situation.

Altering the Fight-or-Flight Response

Speaking to an ex often evokes a fight-or-flight response. One father we watched would get red in the face and clench the arms of the chair until his knuckles turned white. Then he stuttered at the mere suggestion that he talk about what he would say to his ex. Invariably, the first words out of his mouth were, at best, explosive, and at worst, profane.

Beginning a discussion with profanity and name-calling (even if that's the way you feel) is not cooperative. When your blood pressure has already risen or your hands are shaking, you considerably weaken your position. We wouldn't presume to suggest that you can rid yourself of anxiety or rage completely, but you can use techniques that will calm, center, and focus you enough to enable you to stay in control during an argument as well as maintain a powerful position.

Deep Breathing—A Technique That Calms

Breathing deeply breaks into the cycle between your subconscious and your body and gives you an alternative to the fight-or-flight response. When you breathe deeply, you alter the message that your subconscious receives. In essence, you send the message to your subconscious that there is nothing to be afraid of. After all, if there were, you certainly wouldn't be standing around taking time to breath! When you change the message you send to your brain, it stops sending the panic signals that make you ineffective and less resourceful.

To be an effective deep breather, you must practice. Begin by practicing in front of the mirror. Don't rush. Breathe in deeply enough to fill your lungs, then sit or stand straighter and take in just a little extra. Breathe out slowly. Count as you inhale and then as you exhale. Say, "That's one." Breathe again. Say, "That's two." One more time, "That's three."

This technique is useful not only during a conversation with your ex when you find yourself reacting but also prior to phoning or meeting your ex. And if three breaths don't seem to be altering the fight-or-flight response, take more.

Don't Hurry!

When you believe that you must respond immediately to whatever your ex says, and you rush to fill in the silences in a conversation, you inevitably engage the fight-or-flight reaction. In addition, you place yourself at a disadvantage by not allowing yourself time to think. It's not only okay to allow silence (and breathing) in a conversation, it's necessary. If your ex is continuing to talk, or shouting at you to answer him or her, take the phone away from your ear for a moment. If you're face to face, close your eyes. It's difficult to count breaths when you're staring at someone you don't like very much. Closing your eyes momentarily shuts down your visual sense.

If you find it difficult to breathe deeply and incur silence, then practice during your conversations with friends and family members. It may feel awkward at first, but soon you'll discover that the pressure to speak disappears. And remember not to cover your silences with "um." Silence is much more powerful.

Shifting Your Mindset

Part of the difficulty in cooperating with your ex may lie in your tendency to rehearse negative thoughts about him. Much like the self-defeating self-talk we discussed earlier, these thoughts engage and propel you into a negative Think-Feel-Do cycle. For example, you think: I hate him, I hate him, I wish he would die, over and over again as you listen to him tell you why he doesn't have time to take your child shopping for camp. This sets you up to fail because you plan your next action based on these negative thoughts.

Likewise, the self-defeating self-talk you engage in prior to a conversation with your ex sets you up to fail. You may have thoughts like: I can't do this, she's just going to start screaming at me again, or: Why do I even bother talking to him, he's such a jerk. This rehearsal of negative, angry thoughts serves only to make you more, rather than less, angry and negative. That rehearsal robs you of momentum and power and creates a tendency for you to respond argumentatively instead of cooperatively.

Alternative Thoughts

Rather than rehearsing your anger, frustration, or anxiety when you need to discuss something with your ex, write down some alternative thoughts prior to the discussion.

Memorize them, like an actor memorizes lines. As artificial or awkward as it may seem at first, you'll find that just like changing self-defeating self-talk into constructive self-talk, you can create a more powerful position for yourself by rehearsing positive thoughts prior to speaking to your ex. The key is in the rehearsal. You don't even have to *believe* these thoughts. If you rehearse and use them, you'll find they can change your entire composure during a conversation.

To demonstrate, we've listed some common negative thoughts that people have about their exes and a more positive (and thus more powerful) thought to replace them.

Negative Thought: I hate him.
Positive Thought: I can handle my anger.

Negative Thought: What's her problem?
Positive Thought: I'm a good listener.

Negative Thought: He's such a slime bag!
Positive Thought: I'm capable of dealing with all kinds of people.

Negative Thought: I can't stand the sound of her voice.
Positive Thought: I can listen to the content of the conversation and ignore her tone of voice.

Negative Thought: He makes me sick!
Positive Thought: I can handle my uncomfortable feelings.

Negative Thought: I wish I could rip her tongue out.
Positive Thought: I am above physical violence.

Negative Thought: He always puts me down.
Positive Thought: I'm better looking and smarter than his new wife.

Listen to Understand

The basis for cooperation lies in being able to communicate effectively, and the foundation for good communication lies in being able to listen. Steven R. Covey, in his best-selling book, *The Seven Habits of Highly Effective People*, writes that if he had to choose the single most important thing he's learned in the field of interpersonal relations, it would be this: "Seek first to *understand*, then to be understood." Listening and trying to *understand* your ex is far more powerful than you might realize!

Listening is a skill. It's not, however, a skill that most of us were taught, and although we do it quite naturally with the people we feel close to, when we feel confronted, misheard, or wronged, we fail to draw on our ability to listen.

Listening can be broken down into four components: attention, acknowledgment, reflection, and restatement.

The First Component of Listening: Attention

Listening is more than just waiting your turn to speak, more than just being quiet, and more than hearing the other person. The other person must *feel* as though he or she is being heard. We help them feel heard when we give them our full attention.

Giving another person your full attention is a crucial part of the listening process. It means looking your ex in the eyes, keeping your arms and legs uncrossed, and fully facing her. When your body language communicates an attitude of attention, the other person softens her attack, because she no longer feels as if she has to work so hard to get you to understand the points she's trying to make.

The Second Component of Listening: Acknowledgment

Acknowledgment means verbally indicating that you're listening to the other person. That you're actively following along as she speaks. "I see," "Uh-huh," "Mmmm" are examples of how to verbally acknowledge that you're listening. Acknowledging that there is a problem or that your ex has a point doesn't mean that you have to agree with it.

Arthur's ex-wife called him and began to complain about money. She said that she had taken an extra part-time job on Saturdays but was having trouble coming up with money to pay a baby-sitter during that time. Arthur got the feeling that she was taking a roundabout way to ask him for more financial support, which he was unwilling to give. Rather than reacting to his thoughts, however, he simply acknowledged her by saying, "Uh-huh . . . I see . . . I understand that you don't have the extra money for a baby-sitter on Saturdays. It's been a bad year for a lot of us, and eight hours adds up to a lot."

Had Arthur reacted to his suspicions by exploding and saying, "I'm *not* giving you more money. How many times do I have to tell you that before you get it through your thick skull?" it might have provoked an argument, at the center of which would have been their child. Both parents might have left the conversation feeling as though neither of them "wanted" their daughter. Resentment and hurt feelings might have ensued.

The Third Component of Listening: Reflection

Reflection goes hand in hand with acknowledgment. It requires that you try to determine what the other person might be feeling. This isn't easy. As you've already discovered, many times angry words or actions mask our more subtle emotions.

Reflection refers not only to the process of looking underneath the masking emotion for the other person's more subtle feelings but also being able to reflect those feelings back to him. This sounds something like, "I hear that you're feeling defensive about being late," or "Sounds like you feel accused."

When Arthur refused to engage with his ex, she began to utilize some of the old dynamics that hadn't worked in the past. "Arthur, I don't know what I'm going to do. I can't afford a sitter, I just can't." Arthur responded with, "You really sound overwhelmed. Juggling work with a child is difficult."

The Fourth Component of Listening: Restatement

Many times people think they're clearly hearing someone when in fact they are interpreting what's being said.

When Arthur listened to his wife complain about baby-sitting, he was sure that she was going to ask him for more money. Rather than explode at her with, "I'm *not* giving you more money," or "What do you want from me anyway?" he restated what he thought she was saying, "Margaret, I'm hearing you say that you'd like me to cover the child-care expenses for you on Saturdays. Am I right?" To his surprise, she seemed bewildered, "Arthur, I'm not asking you for more money! I was just going to see if we could switch visitation from Wednesday nights to Saturdays so that time is covered for me for the next couple of months."

Asking "am I right?" at the end of a restatement is useful because it enables you to check in with the other person to see if you heard correctly. And it affords your ex the opportunity to correct you if you didn't.

What Can You Agree With?

Another important cooperation skill involves listening carefully to see if there are any points on which you can agree during an argument. Harkening back to our business relationship analogy, when a client is extremely resistant, good businesspeople listen carefully to see if there are *any* points on which they can agree. They think to themselves: Could I agree, either in principle or in part, with any of what she's saying? When they find even a part of a statement they can agree on, they seize that opportunity. It's akin to trying to turn a wild horse around. Sometimes you have to ride the horse in the direction it's going before you can get it to respond to your words and actions.

When you're feeling attacked by your ex, it may be difficult to think in terms of agreement. You're far more likely to enter a negotiation with your ex with thoughts like: She's such an idiot, or: He's 100 percent wrong, as usual! Yet when you look for points on which you can agree, you put yourself in the position of control and relay to your ex that you're working toward a common goal and resolution.

Pulling Instead of Pushing

To better understand how agreement can work in your favor, try this exercise with another person. Face each other and clasp right hands. Both of you push as hard as you can. Feel the way your hands sway back and forth. See how little control there is. Now try it with your partner pushing while you pull toward you. Feel the difference? The same technique applies to verbal fighting. When you agree on some point, it's like pulling your opponent's hand toward you. You now have the control.

Avoiding Communication Blocks

Many times cooperative communication with an ex breaks down because we block it. Sometimes we deliberately do this, and sometimes it's subconscious. It helps to recognize some common ways communication gets blocked: through interrupting, by giving advice, and by invalidating another person's feelings or point of view. Let's see how those look.

Interrupting

Interrupting is one of the most common causes of communication breakdown. In an argumentative state, the thing people want most is to be heard. When you interrupt, you are not allowing the other person to finish his turn. You're not giving him his chance to feel "heard." Remember that cooperation means working together. Let your ex finish what he has to say before you respond, and then request that your ex let you finish, as well.

Giving Advice

Another way to block the communication process is by offering advice. When you become the adviser, the cooperative mood vanishes.

Sam was experiencing some sleep problems at home. His father, Steve, couldn't seem to get him to stay in bed at night until around eleven or twelve. He called his ex, Rachel, to see if she was experiencing the same difficulty on the nights Sam stayed with her.

"Rachel? It's Steve. I have a concern about Sam's sleeping habits and I wanted to ask you a question about it."

"What?"

"Well, I can't seem to get him to go to sleep until around midnight when he's here. I wondered if you were having a similar problem?"

"What you have to do," Rachel sighed, "is be firm. A little firmness goes a long way."

"I am being firm," Steve retorted.

"Well, clearly not firm enough. A boy needs a strong hand, especially from his father."

Steve's blood began to boil. "Are you accusing me of not being a good father? You are infuriating," he yelled, as he hung up the phone.

When Rachel responded to Steve's request for information by offering advice, she may have believed she was being helpful. After all, wasn't Steve asking for advice on getting their son to bed earlier in the evening? The problem is that we often give advice when we're simply being asked for information. To keep communication with your ex cooperative, it's best to determine what your ex wants before dropping your pearls of wisdom. Steve and Rachel would have been better off had she employed her active listening skills, then asked Steve if he wanted advice before giving it. She might have said something like, "It sounds like you're asking me what I would do, is that right?" He might then have responded with, "No, I just want to know if it's happening at your house as well."

Invalidating

Another effective communication block occurs when we invalidate another person's feelings or point of view. Everyone has, and is entitled to, her own opinions and feelings. By telling another person that her opinions or feelings are wrong, or even by implying that they're wrong, you invalidate what to her are legitimate concerns and are more likely to arouse her anger than her cooperation.

Josh's mother, Cheryl, called her ex because she was concerned about Josh using her ex's car during rush hour. She wanted to make the suggestion that Josh borrow the car only before five in the afternoon, when there wasn't much traffic, or after seven, when rush hour was over.

"Hank? It's Cheryl. Do you have a minute?"

"Sure."

"It's about Josh borrowing your car. I'm concerned about him driving in traffic—"

"Cheryl, you're being ridiculous!" Hank interrupted. "Josh is a good driver, and he'll be fine."

"Hank, I'm just trying to ask that you restrict his use of the car to non–rush hours."

"Look, Cheryl, there's nothing to be concerned about. Don't you have better things to do than worry?"

Not only did Hank interrupt Cheryl, he also invalidated what to her was a legitimate concern. Here is a major breakdown in what could have been a cooperative communication between Josh's parents.

The Box Step

Cooperative communication can be looked upon as a box step. Think of yourself as a partner in a dance. What you are doing is drawing a box on the floor by moving your feet in that direction.

1. Step back—and assess the situation. You could, at this point, strike right back, but this action encourages retribution. Listen to understand, and remember that you don't have to make any decisions right this moment.

2. Step to the side—your ex's side. See if there is anything on which you can agree. Look at what your ex's feelings, objectives, and motivation might be.

3. Step forward—present your ideas clearly and concisely.

4. Step to the other side—close your negotiation with a compromise.

Tim's mom was surprised when her ex called one day and began yelling. "You listen to me!" he said, "I am *not* going to have Tim riding a bike in the city. He's done fine up until now without a bike and I think it should stay that way." Remembering the box step of cooperative communication, she didn't engage right away in an argument she knew nothing about. Instead, Sarah stepped back and went into a listening mode.

"I hear a lot of concern in your voice, George. What's going on?"

"Tim says you promised him a bike for his birthday, and I simply won't have it. It's far too dangerous to ride in the city."

Sarah then stepped to her ex's side, trying to hear it from his point of view and find something on which to agree. "I agree that it can be dangerous to ride on the streets." She then stepped forward and presented her plan. "I had thought that I'd buy him a bike only if we limited his riding to the park with a helmet to ensure his safety."

"Oh!" George seemed surprised, almost as if the wind had been knocked out of him. "I guess I didn't realize that."

Then Sarah stepped to the other side, closing the communication. "So can we agree that he can have a bike if he rides only in the park with a helmet?"

"Well, okay," George agreed, "and thanks."

When Sarah engaged George with her newly learned cooperation skills, she was able to handle a situation that previously would have escalated into a fight.

Catch 'Em Doing It Right

One of the most powerful ways to engage another person in cooperation is to acknowledge and appreciate his efforts.

Very often we watch for and pick on the things a person does wrong, mistakenly believing that if we point out his mistakes, it will help the person change his behavior in the future. Unfortunately, this often makes the behavior worse, because soon the person realizes that you'll never acknowledge what he did right anyway, so he might as well do it wrong.

By watching for the things a person does right, however, and acknowledging those things, you increase the likelihood that the person will do things right in the future. Even if you believe that your ex never does anything right, you'll find that it will move you in a more cooperative direction, even if you only acknowledge his efforts: "I know how hard it is for you to get out of the office on time. I appreciate that you made this effort today, even if it didn't work out."

If You Lose It Completely, Apologize

Working toward a cooperative relationship doesn't mean you'll achieve a perfect one. We're all human. Obviously, there will be times when you won't hold it together, when you'll lose your temper or composure in front of your ex. When this happens, apologize. It's not what you do, but what you do afterward that counts. A simple "I'm sorry for calling you names" can go a long way. (This is an important point to remember when dealing with your kids, as well.)

Giving Yourself Permission to Compromise

Finally, cooperating with your ex for the sake of your child means compromise. Many people look at each conversation with their ex as a miniature battle to be won. If you look at it this way, hanging on to your thoughts of revenge, setting out to hurt your opponent, wanting to come out of every conversation the victor, you might end up winning each battle, but rest assured you'll lose the war. Your children are at stake here, and if their self-esteem suffers in your battles, which it most assuredly does, you will have lost much more than you ever realized.

When you give yourself permission to compromise, you give yourself and your children permission to be happy. You've worked hard to get where you are today. Being a single parent is not an easy job. Raising a child is not easy. Cooperating with your ex reflects your maturity, sensitivity, and personal growth and, ultimately, makes things easier for you.

When Your Child
Tops the Problem
Pyramid

Protecting Your Children...

Prior to becoming a parent, you probably had no idea of the strength and fortitude you would need. From the round-the-clock feedings that exhausted you to your child's bumps and bruises that terrified you, each new experience with a child stirs up deep feelings of responsibility.

Most parents, when asked to describe the feelings they have about parenting, say that the guilt, joy, frustration, anger, and love are all overshadowed by the huge sense of being responsible for another person's life. And most parents concur that the intense amount of responsibility involved in taking care of a child can be overwhelming.

Because the responsibility is so huge, parents feel very protective of their children. Whether it involves a hurt arm because he fell or hurt feelings because someone was rude or thoughtless to her, you feel your child's hurt in the deepest part of yourself. You become the mother or father lion protecting your cubs. You roar and rage, hoping to scare the enemy away, and when that doesn't work, you attack, willing to fight to the death to protect your young.

Divorce intensifies the feelings of responsibility and protection that most parents feel for their children, because the parenting partnership, with its daily support and reinforcement system, has been severed. In divorce you see your ex as the enemy, and in seeking to protect your cubs, you attack the other parent. This fighting between parents actually leaves the children feeling unsafe and insecure. Their self-esteem wavers, and because of their egocentricity, they often blame themselves for your fights. In addition, with their parents fighting, they feel that they have no one to turn to, which often results in them turning to their peers.

"I remember when my parents got divorced. It was awful. First of all, I hadn't had a clue that it was going to happen, because my parents were always very private about their fighting. But when they got divorced, the fights suddenly became public. I remember my mother, whom I'd never heard scream before, yelling

*into the telephone at my father, only to burst into tears
when she hung up. And when I stayed with my dad, all
he could do was tell me how unreasonable a person my
mother was and how much I needed his influence so I
wouldn't grow up to be like her. I felt so helpless and
lost. And this went on for years.*

*"When I was in my teens, I really relied on my
peers for support. Unfortunately, at that time everyone
was really into drugs and booze. To be a part of my
peers, I did that stuff too. I've been sober and drug-free
for years now, but I sure wish things had been different.
I really feel like I wasted a lot of years because my mom
and dad were so busy fighting over me that they forgot
to give me the support and protection I needed."*

. . . *At Their Expense*

When we get caught up in protecting our children, it results
in being protective at their expense. Often we take any issue
that our child has with his other parent, any complaint, and
snatch it up as our cause, waving it like a banner as we rush
in to do battle. By taking over in this way, we actually put our
children at a severe disadvantage. Not only do they wind up
not knowing whom to turn to when the issues they have
cause Mom and Dad to fight, but they also lose out on the
possibility of developing some very helpful problem-solving
skills for themselves.

When you are loving and supportive and refrain from
taking over when your child has an issue with your ex, you
help your child feel competent and secure in his or her relationship with *both* of you.

Taking over, on the other hand, makes the child think to himself or herself: Gee, I guess I can't handle things on my own. And with Mom and Dad fighting, things aren't so safe either. If it's unsafe, *and* I can't handle it, then there is nowhere to turn.

With this in mind, it's not only essential to be able to identify when your child tops the problem pyramid, it's vital that you be well versed in the techniques that will help you support your child in solving his own problems.

Listening Neutrally to Your Child

Listening to your child, *really* listening, gives her the sense that what she has to say matters and is worthwhile, that she herself is worthwhile. When children feel listened to, they feel accepted.

Think about how you feel when you talk to your best friend. Your best friend is probably your best friend *because* he or she listens to you. You feel accepted by your friend, and when you leave a conversation with him or her, you feel better about yourself. Why? Because you felt heard and therefore accepted by this person. That feeling of acceptance builds the foundation for high self-esteem.

What Not to Do

The first step in really listening to your child is not in what you do but in what you stop yourself from doing. You must stop yourself from acting on your feelings. This may be especially difficult because your child's ambivalent feelings over something your ex did or said are likely to stir up not so ambivalent feelings within you.

When your feelings become engaged during a conversation with your child, remember that your child's feelings are not the same as yours. Stop yourself from taking on those feelings and becoming enraged in front of your child. Don't allow yourself to leap out of your chair, run to the phone, dial your ex, and scream obscenities at him or her.

This is not to say that you must bury your feelings of anger. On the contrary, if your anger is denied in front of your child, either by being covered up ("I'm fine, nothing's wrong") or outright lied about ("No, honey, Mommy and Daddy aren't angry with each other, it's only a little disagreement"), your child will become confused. These statements of denial refute her own notion of reality because children are very adept at picking up on other people's subtle (and not so subtle) feelings. Children who must deny the reality they see learn to distrust their own feelings. They also stop trusting other people. In short, they will probably be in for years of future psychotherapy!

To get around this tricky issue, if your child picks up on your negative feelings, you can say something along the lines of, "I guess I feel a little angry about that too. But it's okay for us both to have our own feelings. These feelings are normal." You can even add, "Just because I feel angry or upset, it doesn't make either you or Mommy or me a bad person. All people feel angry sometimes, whether they're divorced or not."

Remember that it's okay to have your feelings and acknowledge them, just not to act on them.

What to Do

Once you've stopped yourself from acting on your own feelings, you can adopt a more neutral listening role. Sit still. Make eye contact with your child. Use your deep breathing and calming techniques to objectively hear what your child is saying. Know that what your child may be saying is probably very different from what you're inclined to hear. Your son may be trying to communicate that he's *mad* at his mom, and what you may hear (because you're enraged with her) is that he's *furious* with her. There's a difference between him being mad and him being furious. And he's allowed to feel either way. But they're *his* feelings, not yours. Remember that when you become enraged, you only complicate matters.

You can even pretend that your child is talking about someone you don't know. With your body language (lean forward, incline your head slightly, keep your arms and legs uncrossed), let your child know that you're listening nonjudgmentally. If your child thinks you're judging your ex during the talk, he will do one of several things. Either your child will stop coming to you to discuss these problems, or he will become protective of the other parent. If your child becomes protective, it will distort his feelings and confuse him. Your child might get the message that he is never allowed to be mad at his other parent because it leaves that parent unprotected.

> *"My parents divorced when I was a kid, and I can remember telling my mother about something stupid my father did. The next thing I knew, she was screaming at him about that specific thing. I felt awful. I felt like I had gotten my father in trouble. I stopped telling my mother things after that."*

Protecting one parent from the other is too big a job for a kid, no matter what his or her age. Stop yourself from putting your child in that position. Listen neutrally.

Showing Concern

One thing that helps children feel listened to is restating what they've said in your own words. It's also helpful to interject a feeling word when you do this. In order to not inadvertently block communication, phrase your restatement in the following manner:

"That must have been [difficult, hard, uncomfortable, etc.]."

"That sounds so [frustrating, frightening, sad, etc.]."

"Seems like you're [angry, unhappy, lonely, etc.]."

"I guess [it's difficult sometimes, you're feeling confused, etc.]."

"Sometimes it's [upsetting, maddening, infuriating, etc.]."

What all these phrases have in common is that they convey an air of hesitation on your part. When you come on too strong, you take the risk of mislabeling your child's feelings. You don't want your children feeling obligated to take on emotions that don't belong to them.

"I remember when my parents split up. I was so sad. And my mother kept saying, 'Aren't you angry at your dad?' After hearing this a thousand times, I got angry and didn't speak to my dad for years. It was a bad scene."

When you are hesitant in reflecting your child's feelings, you allow an opening for your child to contradict or correct you. For example, suppose your child said, "I'm not going back to Mommy's house ever again." You might guess that your child felt angry and hesitantly reflect that feeling with, "Gee, you sound kind of angry." If you're wrong, and your child is really feeling embarrassed, he has an opportunity to tell you that. "No, I'm just embarrassed because I got chocolate on her new couch." When your child does contradict or correct you, it's important that you acknowledge the correction with, "Oh, I see, I was wrong. What you really felt was a little embarrassed."

When children are sorting through their feelings, they need to experiment with finding the right feeling word as well as how strongly they feel, and it's important to allow them this self-discovery. If your son, for instance, says, "I hate Daddy," you'll negate his feeling if you say, "No you don't." He may be very angry with his father and saying out loud that he hates him is the way he is able to express that anger. Or he may be annoyed and frustrated at his father and is confusing those feelings with anger. Simply rephrase, deemphasizing the word "hate" by saying, "Wow, you sure do sound angry."

By allowing your child the space in which to explore different feelings, and by validating these feelings, your child will eventually be able to express herself fully, not only to you but to your ex as well.

Brainstorming with Kids

After you've acknowledged to your child that you're listening with your body language and by restating what you heard her say, the next step is to turn the problem-solving process over to your child.

Most of us reached adulthood without ever mastering the skill of problem solving. Yet it is a skill that can open doors, bridge rivers, and literally launch people from mediocre to brilliant careers. Giving our children the ability to problem solve is a gift that will last throughout their lifetime, one they will use in a variety of situations. Fortunately, too, if you help your child learn to solve her own problems, it lessens your contact with your ex, removes you from the divorce communication triangle, and unburdens you as well.

Adults help children look for solutions by asking a series of questions. The first question literally leaves the solution in your child's hands. Phrase your first statement in this way:

"Can you think of anything you might be able to do about that?"

From this basic foundation a variety of similar questions can be formed. The key is that you must not include any suggestions or advice. It's also very important that you don't criticize your child for thinking freely. Even if you know that a particular solution is impossible or impractical, let it ride for now. Here are a few suggestions:

"Is there any way you'd feel comfortable asking your dad about that?"

"Can you think of a way to turn this around?"

"I wonder what you might be able to do about this?"

And if your child responds that she's going to pack her bags and move to Australia, you can say:

"Packing your bag and moving to Australia is one solution. Can you think of another? I'd be very sad if you moved to Australia."

Giving Advice Carefully

When you've posed the initial question, your child may not be able to come up with any solutions or may be able to come up only with ones that you know aren't feasible. Then it's appropriate for you to offer some solutions of your own. This is a bit tricky, however, for a couple of reasons.

First of all, it's easy to allow your own bias and need for revenge to creep in and to offer advice that is prejudiced. Clearly this is a mistake and does more harm than not helping your child at all.

The second thing that makes offering advice tricky is that, as with adults, advice blocks communication with our children, which is the opposite of what we're trying to do here.

I Wonder What Would Happen If...

To offer advice without blocking communication, phrase it as if you're exploring possible solutions to the problem. Instead of saying "Why don't you . . ." or "I think you should . . ." say "I wonder what would happen if you . . ." Like the initial question you pose to your child, this question serves as a launching pad for similar questions that won't come off as if you're giving advice. Here are a few more suggestions:

"I wonder what would happen if you talked to your dad about this?"

"What do you think your mom would do if you . . ."

"I wonder if _____ would work?"

"Have you thought about . . . ?"

Remember that whenever you offer advice, state it in question form, not only to keep the lines of communication open but for a higher purpose as well. If done correctly, this process increases your child's self confidence in problem solving. Because she is not in a position of taking your advice (after all, you asked her what she thought would happen if she took a particular action), she is more likely to take credit if a solution is found. Never mind if that solution came from you in the first place—you don't need the credit for it, you're an adult. She needs credit so that she can more confidently handle issues not only with your ex but also with friends, family members, teachers, and others. (And if your ex is be-having immaturely, try this technique on her, too.)

Handling Negativity

It is naive to assume that this process works as smoothly in life as it does on paper. In fact, more likely than not, once you state your initial question, "Can you think of anything you might be able to do about that?" your child will say, "No! There's nothing I can do." Likewise, if you proceed undaunted, your child will probably reject all of the solutions you pose. This is to be expected.

When this rejection happens (note we don't say "if" it happens), accept your child's feelings. You can say things like, "You sound pretty hopeless," "Sometimes it's hard to talk to your mom," "Mmm, I guess you think that wouldn't work. . . . Sometimes it's hard to come up with an idea." It's also important to add encouragement with words like, "I'm sure if we put our heads together we'll think of something," "You're good at coming up with solutions, and I feel confident you'll figure out a way to handle this to your satisfaction."

It's important to note that this process is not about results. It's not about coming up with solutions. It's about establishing, maintaining, and enriching your relationship with your child. This is a point to be repeated and emphasized. (If we could, we'd lean forward, look intently into your eyes, and gesture emphatically!)

This process is not about results. It's about enriching your relationship with your child! If you become involved in solving the problem, the problem-solving process won't work. It sounds like a contradiction, but it's not. If you stay in the process, it's likely you'll achieve a result, but that's *not* the goal. The goal is to enrich your relationship with your child so that she feels listened to, protected, and supported by you. Keep your relationship with your child, even if your child has negative feelings about you or your ex, in the foreground of this process.

Examining Consequences

Part of problem solving, and indeed of making "good" decisions, involves being able to look at the choices you might be making and what will happen if those choices are implemented. As you know, the results of our choices are called consequences.

When your child tops the problem pyramid, and you engage in listening and supporting him or her in solving a problem, you help your child examine the consequences to the solutions he or she comes up with. Taking your children seriously and helping them explore the ramifications of their decisions ultimately helps them make the best choices they can.

For example, if your child says, "I'm never going to Dad's house again!" help him examine the consequences of that particular choice (even if you know it's an empty threat). You could say, "Well, how do you think you would feel about that?" or "Well, that's one solution. What do you think would happen if you never went there again?"

Let It Rest!

Sometimes questions that help your child examine the consequences of a particular action are met with a response that's either impractical, can't be implemented or both. "If I never say my dad again, I'd feel great. I hate him and his dumb old wife anyway. So I'm never going again."

Rather than jumping for joy or trying to convince your child why she can't choose that, simply let it rest. You can acknowledge her feeling without agreeing. "Well, let's continue to talk about this. I still sense that you're very angry, and maybe we can figure out a way for you not to feel so angry anymore."

It's important to realize that many times a child needs to reject an idea in order to save face, and she will come around very soon afterward.

Allowing Your Child to Have a Relationship with the Other Parent

No matter how you feel about your ex, your child must develop his own relationship with his other parent. This is not an easy process, because you can rest assured that your child has many mixed feelings about your ex. Your child may blame your ex for the divorce; he may resent a new relationship that is developing between your ex and another person; he undoubtedly feels sad, abandoned, and angry; and he probably feels confused about how to have a relationship with two parents who no longer live together.

Allowing your child to develop this relationship, to make mistakes and to achieve successes that are all his own, while still supporting and struggling to understand things from his point of view, is a great gift. So if you feel yourself wanting to intervene, to give advice, to put down or roll your eyes at a solution your child comes up with, stop. Sometimes your intervention causes more problems. And it almost always confuses matters.

Allowing this relationship might also mean not covering for your ex. Sometimes an ex really isn't a very good parent, and all the manipulation you exert won't necessarily keep your child from finding that out. You won't want to make a point of telling your child something that might hurt him, but don't lie if your child asks about it.

"My ex and I were back in court after being divorced for many years because he was seeking a downward modification of child support. It seemed that his salary just didn't go far enough now that he had a new wife and

family. Anyway, he said that he didn't want our son to spend the night anymore, at least until a new child-support agreement was signed.

"Well, the last thing I wanted was to involve Eric in all of this. So instead of telling him, I arranged for him to have something special to do on the weekends he was supposed to see his dad. This went on for about three months before Eric finally asked what was going on and why he wasn't sleeping at his dad's house anymore.

"Then it hit me. It was only a matter of time before my son would figure out that his dad didn't consider him as important as his new family. I couldn't continue to cover. My son deserves honest answers. And if that means that he starts feeling like his dad is a jerk, I'll just have to deal with that."

Handling Aftershocks Ahead of Time

The emphasis in this chapter has been on supporting your child in handling issues with your ex, rather than taking over and making your child's problem your problem. But this doesn't mean stepping out of the picture altogether. After all, you do have the advantage of a longer history with your ex than your child does. Sometimes this enables you to predict how your ex might react in a particular situation with your child.

Your knowledge of your ex's personality can go a long way toward helping your child come up with the best solution to a particular problem. Don't state what you know the outcome might be with a negative phrase like, "Oh, forget it!

Your mom will never go for that. She'll just explode at you and you'll wind up right back where you are now, but with more hurt feelings." Rather, use your information to explore further consequences: "Well, not seeing your mom ever again is something you could choose. (Pause) How do you think she'll react? How would you go about telling her your decision?"

It's important to try and work through as much of the proposed scenario as possible ahead of time. If you know that your ex is likely to be explosive, uncooperative, or simply nonresponsive, yet your child doesn't respond to your questions with, "Well, I guess Mom would really blow her cool and yell at me" (or whatever you know your ex is likely to do), it's important to suggest gently to the child what you think might happen. Again, hesitation on your part creates the impression that you're not trying to be a know-it-all and that you're not against your ex. You might try saying something like, "Well, I have a feeling Mom might respond pretty strongly if you decided you didn't want to see her again. What do you think?"

Handling Manipulation

Like the history that exists between you and your ex, there is a history between you and your child and between your child and your ex. Be aware that your child is very conscious of the different dynamics that exist. Your child may know that you're the "soft" one, the one who gives her what she wants, or that your ex is.

Sometimes this means that your child may try to manipulate you into handling the problem for her. Please understand that we don't intend the term "manipulate" to be entirely negative. All human beings are manipulative at some time or another. It doesn't mean that your child is "bad." What it means is that your child is likely to figure out the easiest route to get what she wants.

Your child may see that the easiest route involves playing one parent off the other, and sometimes she will see that it's easier to get you to argue her case for her with your ex. It's very important to give your child the confidence to confront your ex, since she will have to deal with her other parent for the rest of her life. If you allow yourself to be manipulated into taking on your child's problem, you will, in fact, diminish your child's self-confidence and self-esteem. Your child will feel as though she needs you to rescue her, which only sets her up to remain in a helpless role. In addition, you will enter into that divorce communication triangle with your ex that usually leads to increased upset feelings on your end.

So when you see your child trying to get you to take over a problem that clearly doesn't belong to you, gently reflect how she must be feeling back to her. Say, "Sounds like you're a little anxious about talking to your mom. I can tell you'd really like me to step in."

To boost your child's confidence, have confidence in yourself and convey that confidence to your child. Say, "This is something you can handle yourself. Let's see if we can find a way to make you feel more comfortable when you do." By phrasing it this way, you make it known to your child that you think she can do it, whether she feels comfortable or not.

This kind of confidence goes a long way in supporting children in solving their own problems.

When Your Child's Problem Is with You

Children often become angry with us because as parents, we're in the position of authority. As such, you may need to set limits or boundaries that your children will not necessarily like. Setting those boundaries is a central topic in numerous parenting books. This issue, however, applies to parents in joint custody situations when the child says, "I hate you. I'm packing my toys and I'm going to live with Daddy [or Mom]."

In this statement, it is clear that the child is topping the problem pyramid, but because his problem is with you, it can be tricky to handle. Here are the steps:

1. **Listen neutrally.** This is difficult when you feel insulted, threatened, and fearful that your child might actually choose to go live with your ex. Remember that your child must feel very hurt or upset to be trying so badly to hurt you. Refuse to be hurt, and listen objectively.

2. **Show concern.** Restate what you think your child is saying. Try to determine how he is feeling by watching his body language, listening to his words and tone of voice, and observing his facial expressions. Put yourself in his shoes. How would you feel if it were you? Use feeling words ("sad," "confused," "angry,") to show him that you're concerned and that you under-

stand his feelings. "It's so hard sometimes, isn't it? It must be a little confusing too. On the one hand, you're so angry and so hurt that you are threatening to go live with your dad. On the other hand, you love me. That can be difficult."

3. **Brainstorm solutions.** Let your child know that most topics are open for some discussion. If he can think of anything that would make things easier, he should let you know. "Honey, what can we do about this. I see you seem really mad at me. Maybe if we discussed it, we could come up with a solution together."

4. **Examine consequences.** "What do you think would happen if you went to live with your dad?" This can be a scary question for a parent to ask. What happens if your child actually takes you up on it? If your child were to say, "That would be great! I hate you!" or something along those lines, it would mean that his feelings of anger were still very strong, and it would be appropriate for you to go back into the mode of reflecting feelings. You would want to say, "Gee, you still seem really angry. Sounds like you're still having really big feelings. It's hard." You would want to continue reflecting feelings until you sensed that your child was calmer. Once calm, he is more likely to think through his proposed "solution" (threat). Remember that it's much scarier for a child to change living circumstances than to work things out with you.

5. **Let go.** Let go, let go, let go, let go, let go. Disengage your feelings. Recognize the difficulty your child must be having. Try not to feel threatened. If you refuse to

be hurt and maintain a calm, supportive attitude, your child will eventually wind down and be able to think more clearly. Your child can't hurt you if you don't accept the hurt. Let it go.

The Preverbal Child

A discussion about what to do when your child has a problem wouldn't be complete without mentioning the pre-verbal child. As any parent of a preverbal child who's throwing a tantrum can attest, children don't have to have a language to have problems. Of course, the challenge for parents of a toddler or infant is that you don't necessarily know, nor will you necessarily ever find out, what the problem actually is.

This doesn't mean, however, that you're off the hook. It is just as important, if not more important in many ways, that you acknowledge the feelings your little ones may be having. Because they're not capable of expressing themselves verbally, strong emotions such as fear, anger, confusion, and frustration are usually expressed physically. Your otherwise placid and adorable toddler may hit, bite, scream, and kick when he is feeling a particularly strong emotion. And make no mistake, young children feel the anger and turbulence between you and your ex just as acutely as older children do.

When addressing preverbal children regarding a problem they are having, be attuned to the ways an emotion is likely to manifest itself. In other words, watch for their feelings more than listen for them. Here are some things to look for:

Facial expression. Children may frown, grind their teeth, suck their thumbs or fingers, tense their mouths, clench their teeth, or close their eyes instead of looking at you. By watching your child's facial expression and thinking to yourself what it would mean if you made the same expression, you can draw clues that will help you interpret what your child is feeling.

Body language. Preverbal children who have a problem may avert their gaze, cry, tense their bodies, or clench their fists. They may also become aggressive, biting, hitting, pinching, scratching, kicking, banging their heads. Body language is a good external indicator of internal emotion.

Tone of voice. Listen for pitch and volume. Even without words, tone of voice can indicate strong emotion. Pitch may go up and volume may increase if a child is particularly distressed. Volume may decrease if a child is withdrawing.

By watching the preverbal child's emotional indicators, you can make some pretty good guesses about underlying feelings. And even though your child is preverbal, it is important to verbalize to her what you think her feelings are. (Do this even if she's only a couple of months old. After all, even newborns have feelings!)

When you reflect your preverbal child's feelings, it helps the child learn the words she will eventually use to express her emotions. Even children as young as two have learned the word "frustrated" and are capable of using it properly. In addition, you show your child (through your tone of voice more than the words you use) that someone is in control and is calm. Children who are having strong feelings about something, especially if they're having trouble expressing those feelings, need a parent who seems calm and in control more than anything else. This gives the child a feeling of safety.

You might say things like, "You seem sad," "I guess you're upset with Daddy leaving," "Sounds like something happened that you're frustrated about." Even though these seem like a lot of words for children who aren't using words themselves, it's important to keep in mind that children understand adults long before they're able to express themselves verbally.

While a little empathy goes a long way for the preverbal child, don't think you have to stop there. It's perfectly all right, and even desirable, to continue with the technique and wonder aloud whether there is anything that would help the child feel better, or differently. Remember that *This process is not about results. It's about enriching your relationship with your child!* (Sound familiar?) And if nothing else, you're getting the practice that you'll need when your child does begin to talk!

Staying Out of It

Allowing children to fight their own battles is one of the hardest parenting skills. A parent's inclination is to get in there with the child, to help the child fight the enemy or do the job, to protect the child from harm, and to celebrate victory with the child afterward. But children need to learn how to do this themselves. Just as a two-year-old shouts, "Me-do-it," children fare better when guided and taught to solve problems and finish projects by themselves.

Once a divorced parent learns that many of the problems his or her child is having belong to the child, and then supports the child in solving the problems rather than taking over or taking them on, life is better. Your relationship with your child grows, your relationship with your ex improves, and you may suddenly find that you have a lot of free time that you once spent worrying about how to solve everyone else's problems.

We're not suggesting that you leave your child to fend for himself. We're suggesting that you empower your child with the communication and problem-solving skills that will raise his self-esteem. Then your child will develop a higher sense of responsibility, cooperation, and self-worth. This, in turn, will give your child the courage to confront his other parent, and you will have fewer interactions with your ex!

Onions in the Tuna

Let's look at a situation between Penny and her father. You'll see that Mom originally responds to Penny's problem by taking over but later helps Penny solve it herself.

"Penny was so hungry when she got home from camp the other day, she didn't even say hello before heading for the kitchen. She had spent the night before at her dad's, and at first I thought it was just a readjustment thing. Then as I watched her grab a bag of chips and disappear into her room, I looked in her lunch bag. She had taken one bite out of the sandwich her dad had made for her and left the rest untouched. As I inspected the sandwich, I saw that the tuna he had made was

riddled with onions. I went nuts because I know that Penny hates onions. I called him up and started scream-ing at him, asking him how he could make a sandwich like that for a six-year-old. And you know what he said? He said that in his house, he makes tuna with onions, and that she would have to learn to like it. He makes me furious. We ended up hanging up on each other."

In trying to protect her daughter from onions, Penny's mom, Maria, made the common mistake of rushing in to fix this situation. The problem is that Maria wasn't entirely clear whether this was an issue for Penny. Although Penny hadn't eaten her lunch, and Maria knew that Penny doesn't like raw onions, Maria assumed that it was the onions that were a problem for Penny, when in reality it could simply have been that Penny hadn't been hungry at lunchtime. Remember that when you make assumptions—even if you believe you couldn't be wrong—you often create problems that wouldn't have existed otherwise. Either ask your child if there's a problem or stay out of it, but don't rush in to solve a problem that might not exist in the first place.

Penny's situation didn't end with her parents hanging up on each other. It picked up a week later when she got home from camp. As it turned out, Penny had a problem after all.

"Penny was fine until I mentioned that she should pack to go to her dad's house that night. Then I noticed that she became rather lethargic and started to complain about a stomachache.

"We went back and forth for a while, and finally she told me that she didn't want to go to her dad's house be-cause he cooked 'weird' things for dinner and put onions in her tuna."

When children have a problem that's unresolved, they usually bring it up in some way. If Maria had waited instead of calling her ex, the situation would still have come to light. Of course, Maria's first impulse was to call her ex again, find out what he was cooking for dinner, and remind him that Penny would not eat onions. But this time, she tried a different tack. She began by reflecting Penny's feelings.

"Sounds like you're not real happy about what your dad has to eat at his house."

"Mom, I hate onions. Do I have to go?"

"I did notice that he'd put onions in your tuna salad." Then Mom helped Penny problem-solve, "I wonder if you can think of any way you might talk to your dad about that."

"I don't want to. He might get mad."

"Well, he might. I wonder if we could figure out a way to phrase it so he doesn't get defensive and mad."

"Well, how would I do that?"

"Hmmm, what do you think would happen if you gave him an 'I' message? Maybe you could say something like, 'Dad, when you put onions in my tuna I feel upset because I don't like them.' And what could you ask him for instead?"

"Maybe he could make me peanut butter."

"There you go! Do you think you'd feel comfortable trying it that way?"

"Okay."

When Penny called her dad, the conversation went something like this:

"Hi, Daddy. I'm coming over tonight, right? . . . What are you making for dinner? . . . You know what I really like? I like it when you make macaroni and cheese. . . . Could I please have that tonight? No, I don't like lamb

chops. I like macaroni and cheese. That's all I want, macaroni and cheese. . . . And Daddy, I want peanut butter and jelly for lunch tomorrow. Will you make that for me, please? I can even help you make it tonight. . . . Yeah, I really like peanut butter and jelly . . . and macaroni and cheese. Thanks, Daddy."

While this was not an "I" message per se, Maria had clearly given Penny the tools she needed to feel confident talking to her dad about the problem.

What to Do When Your Child Tops the Problem Pyramid

Let's look at some examples where your child tops the problem pyramid and work through them step-by-step.

Packing

"My ex never bothers to repack my daughter's clothes, schoolwork, games, etc., so that she always makes a big scene when she returns home and realizes that she's missing these things. I'm really tired of buying new hats, dolls, and sweatshirts because her mom can't remember to pack them."

What is the problem here?
"My daughter's things are never returned to my house."

All of her things? And they are never returned?
"Okay. Some of my daughter's things were missing when she came home last time and she was upset. This happens frequently."

(Remember to change your language to keep things in the present and not generalize with "always" and "never." It keeps your issues in perspective, and your feelings will be less intense.)

Who tops the problem pyramid?

Who has the upset feelings? Father and daughter

Who's bringing up the issue? Daughter

Who is responsible for implementing the solution? Daughter

The daughter is responsible for implementing the solution because her name appears as the answer to the first two questions. Another parent, however, might decide that he owns the problem. Maybe his child doesn't care that school-work is being left. But in either case, the solution lies in empowering the daughter to take responsibility here. Let's see how that's done.

The daughter has just returned home, discovered that she's missing her favorite doll, and begins to cry. (We've included the steps of the communication process to help break it down for you.)

1. **Listen.**

   Dad gets down on one knee, looks his daughter in the eye, and says, "Honey, what's wrong? You seem so upset."

   "I left my doll at Mommy's. She didn't pack my doll!"

2. **Show concern.**

   "That's hard. I know how you love that doll."

   "Yes, Daddy, I want my doll. Please will you go get it for me, please?"

"Mmm, you'd like me to go back and get it, huh? I don't think there's time for that today, honey."

"But Daddy! I can't sleep without my doll. Mommy never remembers anything. Please, please go get her for me?"

3. "Can you think of anything . . ."

"I know you're really upset, honey. Can you think of any way you might be able to handle this yourself, because I won't have time to go back today."

"No! Daddy, I need her today."

"It's hard."

4. "I wonder what would happen if . . . "

"I wonder what would happen if you called your mom and asked her to bring the doll later tonight?"

"I can't! Mommy would get mad at me."

"Well, can you think of any way you can get along without her until tomorrow?"

"Daddy!"

"I know, honey. Maybe what we need to do here is figure out how you can best remember to pack your own toys and things so you won't have to go a night without them?"

"I don't know, Daddy. If you'll go get my dolly tonight, I promise I'll remember to pack her next time."

"I'm glad you want to take responsibility for packing her next time. Let's figure out a way to help you remember, and I'll go and pick her up tomorrow."

This dad is on the right track. He has set a firm limit to teach responsibility (his daughter loses the doll for one night, which will help her remember to pack it next time). In addition, he doesn't allow his daughter to blame her mother for forgetting to pack the doll because he realizes that it will be to his daughter's benefit in the long run to take that responsibility herself. He also recognizes that his daughter is developmentally capable of remembering her own things and opens the door to the process of brainstorming solutions to help her remember her things in the future.

Next, he addresses the current issue with a limit (he won't jump in to fix the situation by going to get the doll tonight) but shows a willingness to figure out ways to help his daughter handle that limit for the night. Although no immediate solution was reached, Dad remembered that this process is about enriching his relationship with his child and was patient as well as confident that they could handle this together. He didn't blame, or allow his child to blame, her mother, which would only set him up for possible manipulation in the future.

The Raging Bully

"Nicole called me up crying hysterically the other night after another one of her mother's rages. This one was about Nicole's room. Her mother threatened to throw away all of her toys if they weren't put away neatly. She called her a slob and a pig, and I know it's not really the words that are the problem. It's the way this woman can spit venom that's so frightening. I was at the end of that screaming for many years. So when Nicole calls up and begs me to do something about her mom I feel so helpless. What can I do? Her mom needs professional help but refuses to see that."

What is the problem here?

"Nichole is being verbally abused by her mother."

Who tops the problem pyramid?

Who has the upset feelings? Nicole (and father)

Who brought up the issue? Nicole

Who is responsible for implementing the solution? Technically, Nicole

What are your most intense feelings?

"I feel helpless and terrified that Nicole bears the brunt of her mother's wrath. I'm worried that her self-esteem will suffer."

What thoughts are causing those feelings?

"Nicole's mother is abusive. I hated her screaming at me. I love my child. I can't protect her."

The problem here is now clear, though difficult to solve as well as live with. How can Dad help?

Verbal abuse is difficult to determine, and it's not clear, unless you're an eyewitness, whether the yelling is actually damaging Nicole or simply irritating her. Dad needs to keep the lines of communication open and be supportive, while keeping in mind that he may need to seek professional help for Nicole. In these cases it's better to be safe than sorry by obtaining a therapist or counselor for Nicole who has the knowledge and background to handle this type of situation. That way, if the situation is psychologically damaging for Nicole, the therapist or counselor will be able to make that determination and report the abuse.

Dad might say something to Nicole like, "Honey, I'm going to think about this. I promise that. I'm not sure yet how

I can help, but I'll keep thinking. And next time we see each other, let's talk about it, and I'll tell you what I've thought of. Meanwhile, can you think of anything you might do there? What do you think would happen if you went ahead and cleaned up your toys for now, so Mom will stop yelling. Would that help matters?"

In this way, Dad shows Nicole that he's listening and that her feelings are important enough to him that he's going to continue to think about the problem even when they get off the phone. Meanwhile, he tries to support Nicole in coming up with a solution to the immediate problem. Dad doesn't take over and give advice, nor does he diminish the intensity of the problem by making it seems less important than it is.

Empowering
Your Child

Empowerment = Self-Esteem

There is no question that most children of divorce suffer. One day, the world as they know it changes on them. One parent may move out, or they themselves may need to move. Many of the family rules, from one day to the next, have changed. Their stable and familiar world feels unsafe and uncontrollable.

We're not saying this to make you feel guilty. Children whose parents never think of divorcing can suffer as well. There is a good argument that children whose parents fight all the time and still stay together may be harmed more than if their parents divorced. But it's important to know that when you divorce, and especially if you think your ex is a jerk, that your child's self-esteem and self-confidence can suffer greatly.

When we talk about empowering your child, we're really talking about building your child's self-esteem so that he feels good about himself. An empowered child is one who cooperates, has high self-esteem, can be flexible, and thrives in difficult situations. When children feel good about themselves, they are more resilient, capable, and resourceful. When children's self-esteem is high, they are willing to try harder, reach out to others, and learn from the mistakes they make. Children who have high self-esteem are less likely to misbehave and are more capable of examining choices and determining which choices are appropriate.

On the other hand, if a child's self-esteem is low, she is less likely to reach out to others for support. Many children with low self-esteem do dangerous or risky things. They're less capable of handling the effects of divorce on their lives. They're more likely to give up, to stop trying, and to misbehave. In addition, children who feel bad about themselves, who feel they lack power and control, are more likely to succumb to negative peer pressure.

Numerous things influence a child's self-esteem. How we discipline and communicate with our child, the things peers and other people say and do to our child, and the way our child affects the world around him all contribute to self-

esteem. You can't do much about the way other people inter-
act with your child, but you can certainly do something about
how you handle your own child.

A Word about Discipline

One way that children are empowered is by being disciplined
in a consistent way using limit-setting techniques. If you
aren't consistent in your discipline, if you use reasoning with
your child or spanking your child as your primary discipli-
nary tools, we urge you to find a workshop in your area that
will help you build the vital skill of consistent discipline
through setting limits.

The limits you set for your child increase his or her
feelings of safety and security, and the way you set those
limits affects your child's self-esteem. Children of divorce are
especially vulnerable in this area. They need you to know
what you're doing.

Unconditional Love

The most important component in your child's self-esteem
involves your words and actions that show her unconditional
love. They are the words and actions you use when you discipline (that's why you need to learn limit-setting techniques).
They are the words and actions you use when teaching children to tie their shoelaces, make their bed, or ride a bike.
They are the casual, as well as the formal, words you use
every day to communicate your feelings, wants, and needs.

Saying "I love you" isn't enough to make your child feel unconditionally loved.

In order to understand how to formulate your communication so that the underlying message is one of love, you must first understand why this is sometimes difficult to do.

A Human Being Versus a Human Doing

When your child was born and you first held him in your arms, you probably felt a rush of love unlike any you had ever felt before. There was a bond between you and your child that was based solely on the fact that he existed, on his *being*. He didn't have to do anything, say anything, or feel anything for you to feel this incredible, overwhelming love. This *feeling* is called unconditional love, and it is the basis for self-esteem.

When we love our children for who they are, no matter what they do, and communicate this love in very specific ways, we build a foundation for self-esteem that lasts through all the ups and downs that our children encounter throughout their lives.

Yet there are many times when we confuse a child's *being* with a child's *doing*. At a very young age, we begin to judge our children and to give them feedback on their accomplishments. The unfortunate consequence of this is that our children often feel they have to earn our love by what they accomplish. Then, they never feel good about themselves, no matter how much they do, no matter what their age. Indeed, some adults work outrageous hours, make huge salaries, and always strive to accomplish more and yet are never satisfied, no matter what they have achieved. This is because they were never given the free, unconditional love of their parents, the love that is every child's birthright.

Conveying unconditional love to your child, like everything else, isn't always easy. After all, the world judges your child and expects her to behave in a certain way. And in reality, it's much easier to unconditionally love a human being when she's not doing anything wrong.

Showing your child that you unconditionally love her means learning specific techniques that separate who the child is from what the child does. One of the most damaging things you can say to your child is, "You are stupid and careless. Couldn't you see that the milk would spill if you left it there?" Even if you say, "Leaving the milk there was stupid. Couldn't you see that it would spill?" the child will hear, "Leaving it there was stupid, *therefore*, I am stupid."

The verb "to be" in the past, present, or future implies that the person is "being" a certain way rather than "doing" something wrong. People, especially children, don't hear, "that was stupid," they hear, "you are stupid." And when you attack their being, you damage their self-esteem and they become defensive.

"I" messages are helpful when you must correct a child's behavior, because they effectively separate your feelings about the behavior from your feelings about the child. When you say, "When you leave the milk carton on the edge of the table, I feel concerned because it's too easy to knock it over accidentally. I would like you to clean up the mess, please," your child hears that he made a mistake that you would like him to correct. He doesn't hear that he's a bad person or that he does stupid things.

Listening

As we've said before, listening to your child is a crucial part of building her self-esteem. Children (actually, *all* people) who feel listened to come away believing that what they had to say was worthwhile and that they contributed to the communication. That makes them feel good about themselves.

Listening also has the potential to communicate to your child that you unconditionally love her. Quite often, children blame themselves for the divorce and feel that something they did, felt, or thought caused their parents to separate. They also get confused about their anger at one or both parents and feel even worse for feeling angry. When you listen to your child and accept her feelings, however positive or negative those feelings are, you send the message to your child that you unconditionally love her.

If you could hear your child's thoughts, they might be something like this: Wow, even though I feel terrible, and angry, and really upset, Dad didn't criticize me or give me advice. He just listened. I think he really heard me. I think he must really love me to accept these awful feelings I have.

Confidence

Another important criterion for children's self-esteem is how confident *you* are that they'll succeed—both at things you ask of them (behaviorally) as well as things the world asks. When you act as if you believe that your child is capable of handling situations as they arise, you build your child's confidence.

Yet very often we inadvertently send the message that we expect our children *not* to succeed, either at life tasks or behaving appropriately. This message is conveyed when you say things like, "Don't forget your homework" or "Be careful with that." What your child hears you say is, "I expect you to forget your homework" and "I expect you to behave carelessly or recklessly." One dad told this story. "I was up on a ladder pruning a tree in my yard last year and my neighbor came up to me and said, 'Be careful, don't fall.' I paused for a moment and thought, What does she think I'm trying to do? *Intentionally* fall off the ladder?"

When you look at how these words affect an adult, you realize how ridiculous they are. Yet people use them all the time with children. The problem is that they rob children of their confidence in themselves.

To show children than you have positive expectations about their behavior, phrase your statements in a more positive way. You might say, "I was really proud that you remembered your homework yesterday. I know that you're working hard at being responsible for it every day." Likewise, instead of saying, "Be careful," try saying, "I like how careful you are when you take your plate to the kitchen after dinner."

By phrasing these statements positively, you give your child a feeling of confidence. When children feel confident about their abilities, they are less likely to make mistakes, to be careless, or to forget things.

Letting Go of Ideals

Another way we unintentionally rob our children of their inner strength, and likewise their power, is by clinging to an "ideal" image of them. This image is what we expect our child to be: brave, honorable, loving, beautiful or handsome, good at math, athletic, etc.

For most of us, the image building began before our child was ever born, and this ideal image is usually based on our own childhood. Perhaps you always wanted to be a football hero or a ballet dancer but were never allowed to play ball or take ballet lessons. Maybe you were teased for being taller or heavier than your peers. Perhaps you always envied your brother, who was more athletic than you and excelled at sports.

All of our wishes and unfulfilled dreams, as well as our negative experiences with parents, siblings, and others, go into the creation of what we want our child to be, our "ideal" image of him or her. We'd like him to play football; we worry if she's heavier than her classmates; we wish that he were taller so he won't be teased; we push her in math so she can excel in college and "make something of herself."

Unfortunately, this idealizing sends a message to our children that we have very high standards for them, standards they may never be able to live up to. They hear (sometimes without our even saying a word), "You'll never get it right, there will always be something wrong." Of course, we don't mean it that way. We're really trying to help our children be the best they can be. Nevertheless, the message is a negative one.

How "But" Negates the Words Before It

Accepting our children for whoever they are—fat, thin, tall, short, athletic, or artistic—is not easy to do. The words we use in everyday conversations convey to our children that there are things we don't accept about them. One of the words to watch for is "but."

When you say, "I like how you colored that, but you got a little out of the lines here," you inadvertently tell your child that he is not living up to your ideal image of him. The word "but" negates everything that came before it. So even if you believe you are delivering a compliment with, "You got a good grade in English this time, but your math needs improvement," the child essentially hears only what came after the "but." He or she hears only, "Your math needs improvement," and then adds the unspoken but implied second half of the message, which is "and *you* need improvement too."

Separate Compliments from Requests

To eliminate the word "but" from your vocabulary, separate sentences with a period or the word "and." Even better, separate compliments from requests for behavioral change with a few minutes of time. When you tell your child, "Great job cleaning your room," end there. If you must go on to say, "There are a few toys you still need to put away," let the child take in the compliment fully and have it work toward empowering her. Then say, "Let me help you with the last few toys."

In this way, you still draw her attention to the toys left out, but not in a critical way.

Separate Behavior from Love

Another helpful technique is to separate behavior from love. Instead of saying "What a good boy you are for cleaning your room," say, "Good job cleaning your room." Later you can say, "You're terrific!" when it's not attached to something the child did. This separates what the child does from when he is just sitting around being the great kid he is.

Likewise, instead of saying, "Wow! Great report card," hugging your child, and following it immediately with "I love you," separate the two. Say, "I see you got A's in most of your subjects this time. I know you worked hard. Great job!" ("Great job" refers to the child's behavior, not who he is.) Later say, "I love you" when your child is not doing anything other than just being himself.

Many parents have trouble believing that their child will continue to strive and do his best if they relax and stop watching him every moment along the way. Yet that's exactly what will happen. You must trust that what children need is your unconditional love and acceptance, even if they're having a hard time behaving. And sometimes the most important thing you can do is to get out of your child's way and allow him to thrive.

By letting go of your "ideal child," you'll free her to be herself and allow her to feel unconditionally accepted by you. Mourn the loss of this ideal child if you must, but convey to your child every day that you love her for who she is, not what she does. And trust that your child is trying to be the best she can be, that she will do this more readily without your criticism, and that she usually sees her own faults without you continually pointing them out.

Don't Validate the "Monsters"

Another way we disempower our children and rob them of their self-esteem is by overprotecting them. Of course children need protection in many ways and are dependent on us for various things at different stages of their lives. But we often extend this protection far beyond what our children actually need.

"We divorced when my son was eight, and he suddenly became afraid of the dark. Every night it was a struggle for him to go to sleep. He'd cry and cry that 'monsters' were in the dark and were going to get him. Every night, I was beside myself and ended up staying in his bed until he fell asleep. This went on for weeks. And then he'd wake up in the middle of the night, crying for me to come back, or to sleep in his room. I would go back and forth all night, trying to comfort him. I thought I was doing the right thing by telling him that I could see he was scared and 'I'd protect him.'

"After about three months of this, I finally sought some professional help. A therapist pointed out that although my intentions were good, and that my son was going through an especially rough time, I was actually protecting him from something that wasn't real. By sleeping with him and telling him I'd protect him, I unintentionally validated his monster fantasy.

The message he heard was, 'Maybe there really are monsters, because why else would Mom need to protect me?'"

This child didn't recognize that his mom was responding to his fear; he believed instead that she was responding to the monsters. For our children to feel capable and confident about their abilities, we must support their independence. The mother could have listened to her child's fears and acknowledged them by saying something like, "I know how sometimes things feel kind of scary, especially at night." She could have also provided supportive words that might have addressed the root of the problem—how difficult the divorce was for him.

She might say, "This is a difficult time for you and for all of us. Sometimes when changes are happening, like Daddy and me getting divorced, things can feel a little unsafe and scary." She might then have reassured her son with words like, "It's safe here, and even though you feel scared sometimes, you can know that it's safe." And finally, and perhaps most important, she could have encouraged his capabilities by saying, "I know you'll be able to fall asleep on your own. Can you think of anything we could do to help you feel braver? Would it help if we left the hall light on tonight?"

While it's okay to suggest things that might help her son feel less scared, the only one she shouldn't endorse is staying with him solely because of the monsters. If he suggests it, she might say, "I know you can do it on your own, and I wouldn't leave you anywhere it wasn't safe. Can you think of a way you can feel braver without Mommy staying?" The conversation doesn't need to take too long (too long being more than thirty minutes or so). An appropriate ending, if no solution is reached, might be something like this: "You know, you're good at figuring things out, and I'm sure you'll be able to come up with an idea that will help. When you do, if you need my help for it, you let me know. I'll be right in the next room."

This kind of supportive, problem-solving approach empowers children by promoting their independence. Likewise, it builds their courage because, while you're validating their feelings (in this case, fear), you're not validating the fictitious "monsters." Your child will be left with thoughts like: Gee, it must be okay or Mom wouldn't have left. Also, she must trust that I can handle things myself. I guess I can!

Of course, if the basis for the fear (or other emotion) is valid, for example, if the child is saying, "I'm scared of you and Daddy getting a divorce," you'll want to acknowledge that not only the fear but also the divorce is real. You'll still, however, want to reassure the child by asking what might make him feel safer about it.

With this approach it's also important to know what your child is capable of developmentally. While no child at any age needs to be slept with because she is afraid of monsters (because there are no real monsters), be sure that you provide appropriate support for your child's developmental level.

For example, you don't want to empower your six-year-old to tell his friends about the divorce if he feels afraid to do so. He may not know how, or he may feel embarrassed or overwhelmed by that idea. It may add undue stress to expect that of him. In cases where your child isn't developmentally ready to assume a particular level of independence, you must step in and provide the support he needs.

To know if your child is ready, you not only need to take into account what you know about your child but also check out a book that addresses your child's age. Many times children are far more capable than we give them credit for, and a book about development can provide an independent and objective point of view.

A Shift in Focus May Be All It Takes

There are many times in life when we focus on the negative instead of the positive. Many people spend their lives choosing the "lesser of two evils" instead of the "better of two situations." It's the difference between looking at the glass as half full or as half empty.

Sometimes parents look at their children, and their children's behavior, as half empty instead of half full.

"When I was a kid, every night it was each child's job to rinse her dinner plate and put it in the dishwasher. Night after night, this was the routine, and night after night, I did it. My parents never said a word.

"One night toward the end of dinner, the phone rang and it was for me. Since I was almost finished, my mother allowed me to speak to my friend. I got so involved in the conversation that when I hung up the phone, I had completely forgotten that my plate was still on the table. Well, my stepfather flew into a rage about my 'irresponsible behavior.' I remember thinking to myself at the time that I must have done this for hun-

*dreds of nights the right way, and he never noticed. But
the one time I do it wrong, I'm suddenly irresponsible.*

*"After that, I almost intentionally 'forgot' to put the
dish away, and when I did 'remember,' I let him know
how resentful I was."*

This one incident had a lasting impact on this woman because her stepfather failed to recognize when his stepchild
was doing the right thing and instead pointed out her fail-
ings, robbing her of self-esteem. In these cases, children are
left with the feeling that: Nothing is ever good enough. *I'm*
never good enough. Why should I even try, when trying results in nothing, and only failing is noticed?

Very soon, the child lives up to the "half-empty" expectations and begins to perform only halfway. If the stepfather
had said, "Hon, I'd appreciate it if you'd put your dish away,"
and followed it the next night (when the stepdaughter did
it without being asked) by saying, "You know, I really appreciate how you take responsibility for putting your dish
away without being asked. I may not always mention it, but it
doesn't go unnoticed," this woman would have taken a completely different feeling with her through life. She would
have taken pride in being responsible and for doing things
without being asked, rather than trying to find ways to
"forget" her responsibility and being resentful when she was
called on to be responsible. In addition, she would have felt
closer to her stepfather, as well as supported by him.

To shift your focus, ask yourself these questions.

What has my child done right today?

What can I point out that I admired or was grateful for?

How has my child made me proud today?

Sometimes it takes a little practice to see the glass as half full instead of half empty, but once you begin to look for the positive in your child, it becomes a habit and ultimately helps you look at the bright side in other areas of your life as well.

Be a Role Model

Another important aspect of empowering your child is being a role model. This is usually the part of empowerment that parents find most difficult, yet it's crucial.

Most of us are conditioned (probably because of the way we were parented) to say things that diminish our own self-esteem or to discount positive feedback from others. We say things like, "I'm such a screwup," "I always blow it," "I never do anything right." In doing this, we not only begin a self-fulfilling process for ourselves, but we model for our children that it's okay for them not to feel good about themselves either.

Your child sees this attitude when someone attempts to bolster your self-esteem or courage with a caring thought like, "Wow, I really admire how you're coping," and in front of your child you respond with, "Oh, man, really?" Your child doesn't realize that this is an inappropriate, self-defeating response. She hears this and react similarly when she is in a comparable situation.

In one of our workshops, we do an exercise where the participants give each other compliments. It's fascinating that many people find a way to negate the compliments they receive. One woman said, "I felt jealous of the compliments that were given to the other people. I wanted those compliments for myself." Yet the compliments paid to her were not only valid but enviable: sensitive, open, honest, good sense of humor were among them.

In order to show your children how to let in the good feelings and give those good feelings the opportunity to work toward building their self-esteem, you, too, must acknowledge your strengths and let in the good feelings. By accepting compliments with "thank you" or "I appreciate your saying so," you show an acceptance of your strengths and help your children accept their strengths, too.

When Your Ex
Tops the Problem
Pyramid

Lightening Your Load

When your ex tops the problem pyramid you can't laugh and say, "That's your problem, you jerk! Figure it out for yourself" (even though that's what you want to say). When your children are involved, what you'd prefer to do versus what's best for them are sometimes two different things. Yet often, letting your ex solve his or her own problems is the best route to take. It's how you go about getting him or her to do it that's the issue.

One of the biggest benefits you'll get from deciding that your ex tops the problem pyramid is the load that is lifted from your shoulders. As we've said before, when someone else has a problem, very often we willingly (though many times unknowingly) adopt that problem as our own. We immediately begin thinking about ways to solve it, what we can do, and what we should say. And just as often, the person with the problem is more than happy to hand it right over and allow us to take it. After all, it relieves him or her of the burden.

When Mike answered the phone on Wednesday evening, he wasn't expecting a call from his ex, Jill. She began the conversation without preamble, saying, "Listen, Mike. I know it's my weekend to take Susan, and I'm really sorry, but I just got invited on this great ski vacation that I can't pass up, so you'll need to make other arrangements for her."

"Hold on a sec, Jill," he replied, "I'm in the middle of something. If you'll hang on two minutes I'll get right back to you. Or would you rather I hung up and called you back?"

"No, that's okay, I'll hold."

Mike made a smart move here. By putting Jill on hold, he gave himself a few minutes to think. Very often, when someone is trying to get us to take on a problem, he or she relies heavily on the element of surprise.

Don't Be Pressured into Acting Too Quickly

Pressuring someone to act quickly is a highly manipulative technique. It's an old sales trick to get you to buy before you change your mind, before you have time to comparison shop, to try other brands, or to reflect on whether you even need the item. An ex who pressures you with deadlines is much like a salesperson in this way.

Don't be bullied into thinking you have to give an answer or make a decision *now*. Sometimes the pressure occurs at the beginning of the conversation, as with Mike and Jill; other times it occurs in the middle of the conversation. Whenever you begin to feel pressured, it's appropriate to say things like, "I'm glad I got to hear your side of it. Now I need to think it through and then make my decision." Or, "I know you want an answer right now, but it would be unfair to all of us if I didn't think this through. I'll get back to you in an hour." Or even, "If you want an answer now, it's no. If I have time to think about it, I may say yes."

It's rarely to your advantage to act quickly, and it's usually to your advantage to wait. Using the technique of the immediate no and future yes, as described above, works to your benefit. Except in the rare case of organ donation, you don't have to act as quickly as someone else wants you to.

Mike's Reply

Mike gave himself a minute or two to reflect on what Jill had said, then got back on the phone.

"Thanks for waiting, Jill. Now, what were you saying?"

"I got invited on a ski vacation this weekend that I can't pass up. You know that I haven't had a vacation in over a year, and I really want to go. Now I know it's my weekend to take Susan, but I need you to make other arrangements for her."

"I see," Mike said. "Sounds like this ski vacation is a nice opportunity for you."

"It really is! I'm dying to go!"

"I'll bet! So what were your plans for Susan?"

"What do you mean?" Jill seemed bewildered.

"What alternate arrangements did you have in mind for Susan?"

"Well," said Jill in an exasperated tone, "I thought you could take her. She is your daughter," she added sarcastically.

"You're right, she is," said Mike. "And I'm sorry I can't help you out this time. What other plans do you think might work?"

"Mike! I can't make any other plans. You know I don't have a regular baby-sitter! Why don't you call yours and see if she can take her?"

"It's possible that she's free. Let me give you her number, and you can ask her directly." Mike recited the number over the phone.

"All right, I'll deal with it," Jill replied with disgust. "God, you're impossible."

Mike handled this situation beautifully. He recognized that Jill was trying to hand her problem over to him, and he refused to accept it. Let's look at how he did it, step by step.

Recognizing When You're Being Dumped On

The first thing Mike did was recognize that Jill topped the problem pyramid. The ease with which Jill assumed that he would make different arrangements for Susan, even though it was Jill's responsibility, is reflected in her statement: "I know it's my weekend . . . but *I need you to* make other arrangements for her." When another person makes the assumption that you'll take on the problem, it provides her with leverage and makes you more likely to do just that.

Yet just because someone assumes you'll do something for her, or that she can give you a problem, doesn't mean you have to take it. Have you ever been walking along with your child, and he just finished eating a candy bar or using a tissue, and you suddenly find yourself holding the trash? He handed it to you, and you accepted it without thinking. But you didn't ask for it and you certainly don't want it.

Many exes, as well as other people around you, are more than willing to have you take their problems like a dirty tissue. Remember that these problems aren't being given to you, you're taking them. Mike didn't have to accept the problem, and neither do you.

Listening

The next step Mike took to ensure that the problem remained in Jill's hands was to use his listening skills (sound familiar?). Listening to your ex, of course, is a great deal more difficult than listening to your child. It's especially difficult if your ex, whom you definitely don't like as much as you like your child, is yelling or screaming at you and maybe even blaming you for the problem. But listening, more than any other skill, calms people down and centers them.

Mike began the process of listening by getting off the phone, taking time to collect his thoughts, and bringing down his defenses. Then he let Jill know that he was hearing her by saying, "Sounds like this ski vacation is a nice opportunity for you," and went on to reflect her enthusiasm by saying, "I'll bet [you're looking forward to it.]"

Using Empathy

Acting in an empathetic manner as Mike did when your ex has a problem is an important step in the process of handing the problem back. "What?" you may be saying, "be empathetic with that jerk? You've got to be kidding!" But before you stop reading this book and throw it in the trash, let us explain what we mean by empathy and what it will do.

When we say to use empathy, we are not advising you to *be* empathetic. Rather we are asking that you *act* empathetically. Negotiations between ex-spouses are often stopped before they get started because one or both parties come to the table with angry words and behaviors. When that happens, the other partner, even if he wasn't angry in the first place, often becomes defensive and meets the angry tone and actions with anger of his own. Once both people are acting angrily, a stalemate often results. Both parties end the conversation and often go back to their children to regale them with tales of what a jerk their father or mother is.

When we say to act empathetically in order to disarm your ex, we are, essentially, asking you to make nondefensive statements that should help your ex feel as though you're listening. You want your ex to know that you understand the difficulty he is experiencing, because if your ex doesn't feel understood, *and* he thinks you're refusing to take his problem, he's much more likely to escalate the situation in order to get you to understand. His thought process goes something like this: She must not understand how I feel, and what I want. Otherwise, why would she refuse?

These nondefensive statements make it clear that you understand:

"That's an interesting way to see it."

"So what you're saying is that . . ."

"That's difficult."

"I see."

"I hear you."

"Gee, that does sound like a problem."

"What a dilemma you must be in!"

"I know how hard it can be to [turn down a fun vacation because of the kids]."

Sometimes your ex will go on and on. You think you've made it clear that you understood him, but he seems to be belaboring the point. Here it's helpful to say something along the lines of, "What would help you know that I understand what you're saying? What would you like to hear from me?"

If at any point your ex responds with, "Why are you talking like this?" or "Quit pretending you're a shrink," you may be offering too much concern or empathy and it's time to ease up. Go back to, "Uh-huh," "Mmmmhmm," and other nonverbal but vocal listening cues.

Empowering Your Ex (Why Would Anyone Want to Do That?)

Empowering your ex means turning the tables so that she will think of ways to solve her own problem (besides dumping it on you). You do this, first of all, by knowing what your boundaries or limits are. Mike had other plans for his weekend, and that was a limit he wasn't willing to negotiate. He let Jill know this when he said, "I'm sorry I can't help you out this time," and then he turned the problem-solving process back to Jill by saying, "What other plans do you think might work?"

We support another person in solving her own problems when we ask questions like these:

"How are you going to handle that?"

"I wonder what would happen if you [rescheduled the ski weekend for a time when you don't have child-care responsibilities, brought Susan with you, etc.]?"

"I understand. Can you think of any way to handle the situation with Susan?"

Make no mistake, it will probably take a lot of courage to say these things, especially if you're not used to being assertive. It's difficult to hand a problem back to its rightful owner, especially if the owner is not convinced that it belongs to her in the first place!

Standing Your Ground (It's Really *Not Your Problem)*

Standing your ground essentially means being able to say no to a problem and to stick with it, no matter what tactics your ex uses to get you to change your mind. Jill tried bewilderment ("What do you mean?"), exasperation ("I thought you could take her"), and sarcasm ("She is your daughter"). Mike ignored her tone of voice and responded solely to the content of her statements, which was wise. In this way he refused to be manipulated into engaging in an argument. When Jill said, "She is your daughter," he responded to the content by saying "You're right, she is."

Saying no to your ex or refusing to have your boundaries crossed, especially if you couldn't do this in the marriage, takes some practice. But, like the other techniques in this book, it soon becomes second nature. If saying no is your problem, start today with a little no.

"No, I'm sorry, I can't do that."

"No, I'm sorry, I won't be there."

"No, I'm sorry, I'm not interested."

"No, I'm sorry, Madonna's taking a few of us dancing tonight.

Two More Tips

Do Unto Others . . .

Another thing Mike did right was treat Jill in a respectful way. A polite attitude bolsters your self-confidence and self-respect, even if you are walking on a one-way street. Speaking to your ex as adult to angry ex gets you farther than speaking as angry ex to angry ex.

Watch Your Tone of Voice

Tone of voice often carries more meaning than the words you use. By keeping your tone of voice calm, firm, and respectful, you convey an attitude that you mean what you say and that your limits are nonnegotiable. Although Jill had a few parting words for Mike, "You're impossible!" she ended up taking back her own problem.

CLICK!

"I knew my ex ran from problems, but it really became evident after we separated. We were arguing a lot over money, visitation, parenting, all the usual things, and she started to hang up on me. I'd be right in the middle of telling her why I thought she should or should not do something and I'd hear CLICK! It was so annoying that I would call her back and shout obscenities and then hang up on her."

Sometimes your ex is so intent on avoiding her problems that she simply hangs up on you in the middle of the conversation. Banging down telephones, slamming doors, and even uncontrolled raging effectively cut off communication between you and your ex, and your ex knows it. When your ex clicks the phone or slams a door, your first reaction may be to retaliate. "You jerk, how dare you . . ." But this is not the most effective way to handle "clickers" or "slammers." It's better to hold back your response and redirect your reaction. Yes, you may be so angry that you want to scream at your ex. So call a friend instead and vent in a healthier way. Then give your ex, as well as yourself, some time to cool off before you call back to renegotiate the solution to the problem.

Claiming the Top of the Pyramid

When your ex does cut off communication abruptly, it may be necessary to deal with the issue as your problem, regardless of who originally topped the problem pyramid. Not fair, you say. And you're right. But remember that the goal here is to keep your children out of your conflicts so they're not hurt in the divorce process. If that means you need to formulate an "I" message and choice, and call your ex back, do it. It will stand you in good stead in the future.

When the Problem Is So Big That You Need Legal or Professional Help

If your ex continually abdicates his or her visitation responsibilities, continually harasses you, continually mistreats your child, or continually misses child support payments, you may need to seek professional help. Notice that we use the word "continually." Occasional behaviors may go away by themselves. But when occasional behaviors become commonplace, stricter measures must be employed.

If you need a therapist, find one. If you need a lawyer (or a better lawyer than you have), find one. If you need the police, *call them, now!* If it's your ex who needs the therapist, you can suggest seeing one together, but don't get your hopes up. Sometimes the most you can do is send him or her a copy of this book and hope he or she reads it.

Finding a Counselor or Therapist

If you really believe that your ex needs help, you might suggest joint counseling for "parenting issues." But if your goal is to get your ex into therapy for his or her own good, give up. The only person you can change is you. Finding a therapist or counselor for yourself will help you deal more effectively with the feelings that come up in connection with your ex.

For some people, the thought of seeing a therapist or counselor evokes some sort of shame, but in reality, therapy and counseling are more like taking a course in "self." Think of therapy as a map to life. Most of us eventually find our way, but looking at a map or asking for directions makes the process much easier.

Other people hesitate to call a therapist or counselor because they feel that seeing one is a lifelong process. The truth is that if you like the process (and the results), you can make it lifelong. But if you prefer to set a time frame, most therapists or counselors are willing to work within it. Say, "I'm having a hard time with my ex right now and I'd like to spend three months [or six or twelve months] exploring what I can do to make this process easier." If the counselor or therapist you speak to doesn't like time frames, you can find someone else. It's also important to make sure that the therapist or counselor you choose is specifically trained in divorce and stepfamily dynamics and in communication skills.

Whether you decide to go into counseling is up to you. We do recommend, however, that you seek professional help immediately if you notice that your children are suffering. This may mean therapy for your child, for you, or for both of you.

Signs that your children need professional help include poor school performance when it was good before, unusually aggressive or lethargic behavior, excessive weight gain or loss, mood swings that range from extreme hostility to overt affection, and uncharacteristic and intense tantrums and overreactions. Negative changes in your child's behavior, such as lying, cheating, stealing, or drug or alcohol use are also signs that your child is having a hard time. Remember, too, that not every behavior and emotional problem that a child experiences is a direct result of the divorce.

Kids are resilient and can survive divorce, along with most other family crises, as long as they have a supportive home environment, a sense of structure in their lives, and genuine caring from at least one parent. If your child is reluctant to go to therapy, see a therapist yourself who can help you work through specific issues with your child.

When Your Ex's "Other" Tops the Problem Pyramid

The Case of the Wimpy Stepfather

There will be times, after your ex has formed a new relationship, where you may find that a problem seems to belong to your ex when, in fact, he is actually acting under pressure from his *present* spouse or significant other. Consider Sam's story.

> *"Whenever our son gets even a minor illness, my ex starts rearranging the visitation plans. It's as if she doesn't want him to spend the night, or have contact with her new husband, but she still wants to see him. So she'll call me sounding desperate and ask if she can just take him for the day, to the zoo or to the park, and return him before dinner. Or she'll ask if she can take him for a few hours to a movie instead of overnight. I really think her new husband is behind this. He's got a high-powered job and seems absolutely paranoid about getting sick and missing work. I want my ex to see our son, and she does too, but one time she even wanted me to rearrange visitation because I mentioned that our son had athlete's foot."*

This type of problem is the most difficult to sort out. Because it has a snowball effect, where one person passes a problem to another, who takes it on and passes it to you, it's often difficult to see where the problem originates and which parties need to handle it. If we could go into the home where the problem originates and be a bug on the wall, listening in, here is what we could break the situation down to:

Who tops the problem pyramid?

Who has the upset feelings? New husband

Who brought up the issue? New husband (tells wife he doesn't want her kid around because he might get sick)

Who is responsible for implementing the solution? New husband

But what *really* happens at this point? The wife has a problem because she wants to see her son, but she also wants to accommodate her new husband. Rather than standing her ground with him, she comes to you and it breaks down this way:

Who tops the problem pyramid?

Who has the upset feelings? Your ex

Who brought up the issue? Your ex

Who is responsible for implementing the solution? Your ex

If you allow this problem to remain between you and your ex, you'll wind up frustrated, angry, and constantly having to change your plans. This is where you have to allow your ex to handle the problem with her new husband. Accommodating her screws up your plans and allows this pattern of behavior to continue.

With this new insight, let's see how Sam handled the situation the next time Robin called.

"Sam, it's Robin. How's Danny doing?"

"Fine. He's had a little sniffle recently, but he seems to be getting over it."

"A sniffle?! Do you think it's contagious?"

"You sound concerned," Sam replied, using his empathy techniques.

"Well, no," Robin hedged. "I mean . . . well, anyway, um, I guess I was wondering if I could just have Danny during the day Saturday. I'd like to take him to the zoo, but something's come up for Saturday night and so I don't think I can have him over for the night."

"Is there something I can help with, Robin? I hear a little hedging in your voice. Is there a problem with Danny being sick that I don't know about?"

Sometimes an attitude of sympathy can help you get to the bottom of a problem. In asking first if he can help, then reflecting the feeling he heard in Robin's voice, Sam is more likely to get to the root of the problem.

Robin replied, "Uh, no. I mean, well, it's just that Mark has an important project coming up, and he can't afford to get sick. So I thought I'd just take Danny to the zoo so Mark wouldn't catch whatever he might have."

"Oh, I see," said Sam. "It sounds like Mark is concerned about getting sick and missing work, and that's why you haven't been taking Danny when he's not 100 percent. Is that right?"

Here, Sam simply restated the facts, then checked in with "Is that right?"

"Well, yeah," Robin admitted. "I just feel kind of stuck, because I really want to see Danny."

"I guess you must feel kind of stuck. After all, kids always have some kind of minor ailment, and Danny's been no exception this past winter. Sounds like it's hard on you to be missing out on so much visitation. I guess you discussed the fact that Danny isn't always contagious."

"Well, sort of . . ."

"I wonder what would happen if you pointed that out to him. If his only objection about Danny spending the night is when Danny's contagious, maybe he'll be willing to have him overnight if he knows he's not. Or maybe it would be easier for you if I didn't tell you about every minor thing Danny's had recently."

"Maybe."

"This sounds like a difficult issue for you, Robin. Why don't I go ahead and plan on not mentioning Danny's health unless he's contagious. That way you don't get caught in that bind."

"Well, okay, I guess. But what about Saturday?"

"It happens that I can keep Danny on this particular Saturday night, although I'd like you to tell him yourself, so if he's disappointed you can handle it."

"Okay, and thanks, Sam."

Sam did a good job here of handling the problem. Although it still may appear that he took it on (because he's keeping Danny on Saturday night), he made what might possibly be great inroads for the future. Finding out what Robin's real issue is enables him simply not to mention Danny's health to her unless it's serious. Meanwhile, he's made the subtle suggestion that communication with her current spouse might be beneficial to everyone concerned. In addition, he's made it plain that she'll have to handle their son's potential disappointment herself, which might ultimately serve as a motivator for her to stand up to her new spouse.

This conversation represents an awful lot of work for Sam (though not as much work as having a screaming fight with Robin), but he's clearly kept his number-one priority in mind—Danny. It's in Danny's best interests for Sam to spend extra time and effort to encourage his ex to look at solutions to this problem. While it may seem as though he's almost serving in the capacity of therapist (which is *not* appropriate, by the way), the communication remained short. Had things dragged on and on, had Robin been unwilling to look at solutions or admit there was a problem, Sam simply could have stood firm about his boundaries and left Robin to figure out for herself how to handle a sick child with her new husband.

For example, he might have said, "I can see your problem, Robin. It sounds as if Mark is very worried about catching something. But I have made other plans and Danny is not that sick." That's definitely the shorter route, but sometimes it's in the child's best interests, especially when the problem is recurring, to take a little extra time, probe a little deeper, and try cooperatively to arrive at a solution.

The Role of the Stepparent

This is not primarily a book about stepparenting, but it is appropriate to say a word about the role that stepparents can play when they're married to someone who has joint custody with a jerk.

Being a stepparent is a difficult and often unrewarding job. Think of all the fairy tales where the stepparent gets a bad rap and you have a not too unrealistic picture of society's view of stepparents. Yet the bad press that stepparents get is, in the majority of cases, unjustified. Stepparents can be a loving, supportive, understanding presence that enriches a child's life immeasurably.

If you delve beneath the surface of those fairy tales, you can see the difficulties that stepparents face. The doting biological parent ignores the misbehavior of the children, creating more work for the stepparent, who feels left out, resentful, and angry at the "raw deal" she or he was dealt. After all, the stepparent fell in love with another adult, not the stepchildren, yet they always seem to be around, interfering with the marriage. Likewise, the biological parent isn't always approachable about the subject.

In cases where the parent has joint custody with a jerk, the issues are complicated for the stepparent. Not only does he or she have to deal with the children, he or she has to deal with the ex (in absentia) as well. While the ex may not be physically present, the ex who is a jerk makes his presence known, as he lives on (psychologically) in the daily life of the parent. A stepparent is then dealing not only with the reality of someone else's children but also with his spouse's frustration, anger, helplessness, and complaints about the ex. Many times it feels as if the ex is actually living with the new couple. In addition, the mistakes that ex has made with the children take their toll, because the children very often act out, misbehave, and have a lack of consideration for the rules in the stepparent's home. Consider the following:

"My husband's son, James, who is seven, came to visit us. We have two children of our own, five and three years old. Well, the first few days were okay, until we got together with a group of friends who have children. My husband was at work and I had all three kids. James picked up a stick in the park and was swinging it

around. I asked him to please stop, because I was afraid he might hurt someone, and he said, 'Good! I'll hit 'em all. My mom hits me, why can't I hit them?'

"Well, I was shocked. My husband and I don't believe in hitting our children. So later I asked James to tell me what he meant, and he shrugged and said, 'My mom has to hit me 'cause I'm a bad boy.' I said, 'James, it must hurt your feelings when that happens.' Well, it was like I'd opened a Pandora's box. He began to sob, and all this stuff came pouring out. He said, 'I'm bad. Mommy hits me when I'm bad, but there's no one there to protect me. You're not supposed to hit people, but Mommy hits me when I'm bad. I have to go,' and he started to walk away from me. I said, 'James, let's talk about it,' and he said, 'No, I can't be around people when I'm upset. My mommy doesn't let me be around people when I'm upset because I'm a bad boy.'

"I have to tell you I didn't know what to do with all this stuff this poor kid was suffering with. I tried my best to just be sympathetic, but it was difficult to get through. The rest of the day was awful. James had a lot of anger and it just came pouring out. By the end of the day, my kids were a wreck and so was I. And truthfully, I began to lose some of my sympathy when it started affecting my kids. I mean, who was this woman who had so much power over all our lives?"

This kind of scenario is not unusual. Very often, the stepparent is placed in a position of being a confidant to the child and, as in this case, in the awkward position of protecting her own children from the stepchild. What the stepmother did next, however, shows insight and skill in handling the situation with her husband.

> *"When my husband got home, I decided to let him have some downtime instead of coming right at him with my concerns. I'm so glad I did! Between the time he got home and the time the kids went to bed, he had already experienced some of what I had during the day. All three kids were clingy and needy, verbally as well as physically picking on one another.*
>
> *"It was so unusual for our kids to be that way that my husband asked me what was going on. I suggested that we wait until the kids were in bed to talk, and he agreed. When we sat down later, I told him that it looked like he was concerned (instead of focusing on myself), and he brought up the children's behavior. Rather than get defensive about our kids being included with his (since I saw James as the perpetrator), I simply relayed what James had told me earlier about being hit.*
>
> *"Well, my husband was equally shocked—and furious at his ex as well! It provided a really good entry to a discussion that might not have been possible if I had exploded about the tough day I'd had. It was worth keeping my feelings to myself for just a little while, because my husband was much more open to hearing them after I told him about James in a sympathetic way."*

When your spouse's children are with you, schedule routine talks with your spouse. And let him or her air feelings first. Whenever possible, try to be empathetic about your stepchild's behavior, recognizing that often the behavior is a result of the ex.

"I have to say, our discussion went on for a long time, and I tried hard to see my husband's point of view, because he did feel defensive at times during our conversation. I tried to focus on his feelings, and truthfully, he was equally concerned about the impact that James was having on our kids. I told him what I wanted, too, that his ex needed to be approached about her parenting because it was so obviously affecting James (I tried to keep our kids out of it, even though it was hard). I could see that my husband was feeling a little overwhelmed, so I gave him a concrete suggestion about how to approach her."

When possible, avoid simply airing your feelings without having a plan of action to suggest. In all likelihood, your spouse is also feeling overwhelmed and needs specific suggestions for what to do.

It can be very rewarding to act as a team. Don't make it "our kids" versus "your kids," or your spouse will become protective and close off communication. Call a professional for help if you get stuck.

The primary role of a stepparent is to be part of the solution, not part of the problem. Read Chapter Seven, "When Your Child Tops the Problem Pyramid," for supportive techniques that won't put your spouse on the defensive. These techniques are appropriate to use with your stepchildren (and your biological children) as well. Remember that you can take your feelings to a friend or counselor, but the most effective way to get through to your spouse is through teamwork, not a "me versus you" mentality.

Divorced Homes Are
Different (Sometimes)

Your Family Is Unique

As you begin to negotiate your way toward a healthy divorced lifestyle, it's important, perhaps even crucial, to let go of your expectations of what your family "should be" or, more importantly, "could have been." The road ahead is not the one you thought you would be on, especially alone with a child in tow, but it is where you are. If you accept that you can go anywhere from where you are, you're off on a new and exciting journey.

Divorced homes are unique, and an acceptance of that uniqueness can help you structure your "new" family (with or without another adult) so that all its members—whether there are two of you or ten—not only survive but thrive in their new family unit.

Consider yourself one of the lucky people: You have a child to journey with. Your child may be a lot of work right now, but as she or he grows, the physical work required to raise this child will lessen and the pleasure you receive from him or her will grow and deepen. As your child gets older, most of your problems with your ex will diminish too.

And Sometimes Divorced Homes Aren't So Different After All

It's understandable that you may feel overwhelmed at the thought, as well as the reality, of raising your children single-handedly. Maybe you feel devastated at the thought of *not* seeing your child every day. It would be very natural for you to attribute the various problems that arise as your life unfolds to the divorce. Yet many problems that will come up for you are no different from those that come up in intact families. After all, children are still children, and parents are still parents, whether they're raising children separately or together. Your divorce is not the cause of your problems, only a contributing factor to the daily challenges that parenting presents.

By recognizing that some of the issues are ones you would face anyway, you can help yourself feel less overwhelmed.

> *"The mornings are the worst. I plop my son in front of the television with a dish of Cheerios while I take a shower with the door open so I can check on him every few seconds. After I get dressed, I try to get him dressed, which is usually a battle. He won't put on his socks. He won't wear this. He won't wear that. By the time I drop him off at preschool and get to my office, I'm exhausted."*

Sound familiar? That quote came from a happily married mother of two. Her husband gets up one hour earlier to take their older daughter to school. Even for them, parenting is difficult at times. It's exhausting for nearly everyone with young children. And it is even harder when you have to do it alone. But as your child gets older, these situations will change and many of the difficulties will disappear.

> *"I wake my daughter up at six-thirty every morning. Sometimes she doesn't get up right away, but she has her own alarm that goes off at six forty-five, and she knows that if she's not up by then, I'll miss my train. After I wake her, I take a shower and she gets dressed. While I get dressed, she makes herself a sandwich that she eats in the car on the way to school. She has to be there at eight. I drop her off and catch the eight-fifteen train. It wasn't always this way, and boy, am I glad those other days are over. I feel badly that my wife, who deals with our son each morning and drops him at preschool, has it so much harder than I do, but that will change in time, too."*

This was said by the happily married husband of the woman in the previous quote. The truth is, *all* parents know the physical work and scheduling challenges that having children presents.

What Parents Fight About

Divorced parents haven't cornered the market on disagreements, but they certainly have their share, with their primary discord relating to the issue of money. Many divorces proceed amicably as long as the monetary agreement is acceptable to both parents. When it becomes unbalanced—when one parent needs more money or the other offers less, or if your child incurs unexpected expenses—your ex can turn into a jerk in a second. And unfortunately, money problems usually do arise at some point simply because it costs between 30 percent and 60 percent more to operate two households than it does to run one. Often, too, one parent resents the other for having more money or feels taken advantage of for having to pay more.

When money issues arise, it's critical that you keep your child out of the argument. To do this, you must first recognize that you're putting her in the middle. There are many subtle, as well as overt, ways parents do this. Consider the following.

"My daughter wanted sneakers for her birthday that cost $119 and I just couldn't afford it. She kept nagging me and dragging me into the store to see them. Finally, one day, I just burst into tears and started sobbing that

if her dad gave us more money, I could buy things like that for her."

This mother subtly engaged her daughter in a money conflict with her ex. By implying that her ex was responsible for her inability to purchase the sneakers, she was essentially blaming him for not meeting their daughter's "needs." Let's see what she had to say after she'd thought about it a little more.

"Later, I realized it wasn't that I needed more money from her dad. I just needed more money. I remembered back to when our daughter was younger, when my ex and I were still married. I didn't have $119 to spend on sneakers back then either."

This mother came to the realization that with or without her ex, this type of problem might still occur, and dragging her ex into it was very unfair to her daughter. Had she said something like, "Honey, $119 is a lot to spend on sneakers. I'm not comfortable spending that much. Is there any way you can think of to save or earn the money?" she could have avoided involving her ex.

There are also very overt ways we engage our children in money conflicts. For example, it's really easy to answer a child's request for something with, "Ask your dad to buy it for you" or "Doesn't your mother take care of these things?"

"Tommy had his heart set on a bicycle for Christmas, but my cash flow was really tight. I tried to explain that it might have to wait, but he just said, 'It's okay, I'll ask Santa. Then it won't cost you anything.' I felt terrible. I could tell it was his heart's desire. And in his letter to

Santa, he wrote, 'You don't have to bring me anything else, Santa. All I want is a new bike and I'll be happy.' I knew that I wouldn't be able to manage it this year, but I wanted so badly for him to have it. And then as I thought about it, I got angry. Why couldn't his father buy it? He had plenty of cash. I'm afraid I blew it, because when Tommy asked me if I thought Santa would bring it to him, I exploded and said, 'Why don't you ask your father? He's the one with all the money. Ask him to get it for you.'"

This is a terrible setup. Not only is the child left wondering what he did to provoke the anger, but by passing the buck (pun intended), this mother has set it up so that in the future, Tommy will be hesitant about expressing his wishes and desires to her and may look at Dad as the approachable one. In addition, Mom needs to consider whether she wants her son to get the material things he asks for whenever he asks.

It's far better to be honest with your child about money, saying that sometimes we have to wait for things that are expensive, even if we really want them, and that even Santa can't always bring children what they want exactly when they want it.

Many times the money conflicts arise because parents worry or feel guilty that they can't provide for their kids as well as their ex can. Maybe he's always taking the children to Disneyland, or she has a bigger house with a pool, or he just bought them rollerblades. This can be hard to swallow, but children are very good at differentiating between emotional support and material gain. Children know when their affections are being bought.

*"I grew up in a divorced home, and whenever my mom
wouldn't buy me something I wanted, I'd call my dad.
He usually came through for me because back in those
days, he had more money. I didn't think that he was
nicer or better than my mom for doing it, though. I just
used it as a way to get what I wanted. He used to buy
me big presents for Christmas and my birthday, too,
and my mom always used to accuse him of trying to buy
my love. But you know what? I saw through it all.
Yeah, my dad bought the dolls and bikes and cars, but
my mom was there to help me with my homework."*

Different Parenting Styles

All parents, whether they're in an intact or divorced family,
have conflicts because of different parenting styles. One
parent thinks television rots children's brains; the other
thinks it educates and entertains them. One parent sees that
the child stays away from refined or processed sugars; the
other is on a first-name basis with the dinner crew at Mc-
Donald's. One parent never leaves the child unattended; the
other believes that time alone builds character and sharpens
survival skills.

Different parenting styles cause disputes over scheduling, priorities, attitudes, permissiveness, money, discipline,
food, health, safety, routines, and more. Because you most
likely have lost respect for your child's other parent, behaviors and attitudes that might originally have simply been attributed to a difference in your parenting styles can now
become major issues that add fuel to your fire.

"My ex makes our son wear a hat whether it's cold out or not. Josh is like me and hates hats. It's getting to the point where he doesn't want to go to his mom's house because she makes him wear a hat. None of the other kids in his class wears a hat. He's now five years old and I think he should be able to decide for himself if his head is cold, but I just can't get through to his mother about this. It's becoming a major issue for us."

Just because your ex doesn't parent the way you do or the way you want him or her to, doesn't mean he or she is wrong. Parents in strong, healthy marriages often differ on subjects like whether your son can put a hole in his earlobe or whether your daughter can put a third hole in her earlobe. Keep these stylistic differences in perspective and empower your child to deal directly with your ex.

Creating a Different Structure

By recognizing the ways divorced families are different from intact families, as well as the ways they are the same, you have an opportunity to create a different structure for your "new" family. This new structure will provide a good foundation on which your family can grow. Your divorce requires that you formulate different guidelines for appropriate behavior.

Accepting That There Are Different Rules for Different Homes

When a man and woman marry with the goal of forming a healthy family unit, individual styles of everyday living merge into a common ground. *His* way and *her* way become *their* way of doing things. When they divorce, their way often reverts to his way and her way. Parents may worry that this is confusing for kids, but children can rather easily accept having different rules at Mom's and Dad's house—*as long as they are not asked to choose which is better.*

> *"My daughter used to complain that her dad wouldn't let her drink soda at his house. I thought it was great that he could enforce that. So when she complained, I just empathized with her, saying things like, 'Gee, it must be tough not to have soda all weekend.' After a while, she stopped complaining about it. I think the fact that I accepted that her dad would have different rules made it easier for her to accept it too."*

Children will adapt to nearly any rule or routine as long as it is consistently enforced within that particular household. Eating only health food at one parent's house or reading for an hour before bed at the other's becomes the standard for that house. While it may be hard for *you* to accept, doing so will help your child adjust far more rapidly than if you resist.

Don't Make Your Child Choose Sides

Children want and need a relationship with both of their parents. When they're asked to take sides in the divorce, to choose who is better, who is right, or who is wrong, it places them in a vulnerable position. They wind up feeling disloyal and resentful. As it is, even if they're not asked to choose, many children feel that loving one parent (or a new stepparent) is being disloyal to the other one. Your children need your verbal permission to love and care for your ex, even though you no longer do.

It's also critical to acknowledge to your child the importance of her other parent. Having a parent move out can be emotionally devastating. If you create an even bigger distance between your child and her other parent by getting in the way of their relationship emotionally, it will take your child much longer to adjust to the divorce. If the emotional distance between you and your ex is fueled by anger, your child may pick up on that and carry that anger into her adult relationships. Encourage both visitation and interaction between your child and her other parent, no matter what your feelings for him or her are.

One of the reasons parents intentionally or unintentionally distance their child from the other parent is that they're seeking assurance that getting divorced was the right thing to do. In making your ex the bad guy in front of your children, you may subconsciously be trying to get them to support your decision. Even if you truly believe that you were wronged, make a strong effort to dispel any kind of blame. Divorce happens. It's not a "fault" situation. It's a life situation. Don't make your children prisoners of your war. Don't ask them to contribute to your battles. They have a right to their own relationship with each of their parents.

No Confiding or Keeping Secrets

One of the worst things you can do to your children is ask them to keep a secret from the other parent. This puts them in an untenable position. If they keep the secret, they're being disloyal to the parent who doesn't know. If they do tell, they are betraying the trust of the parent who asked them to keep the secret. It's lying in reverse. To ask a child to withhold any reference to something he did, saw, heard, or experienced is asking him to lie. Not only will it weigh on his conscience, but it sets a precedent for lying to you as well.

If you are doing something that you think your ex might object to, tell your ex yourself. Don't let your children take the heat. It's not fair.

> *"My parents offered to take my son and me to Disney World for a much-needed vacation. But it would mean that Todd would have to miss a few days of school. I knew his dad would go nuts over the school issue, and he would scream at me. So I sent him a note instead of calling, two weeks before we left. That way, he would have some time to 'cool off' before I had to face him directly. It also removed Todd from the conflict and gave him the freedom to talk openly about the trip."*

Don't Kill the Messenger or Reward the Spy

Don't ask your child to carry messages to or from your ex. When arrangements have to be made, call your ex directly or use the mail or fax. If your ex is sending you messages via your child, tell him or her to stop. If this doesn't work, empower your child to say no to your ex with a simple, "Please, Mom, if you have something to say to Dad, do it directly. Don't involve me."

> *"I had to tell my mom that my father was getting remarried! It's thirty years later and I'm still furious at being the messenger."*

Sending messages through your child is not only unfair to your child, it opens the door for mixed messages, incorrect messages, and all sorts of manipulation.

"For a while, I wasn't speaking to my ex so I had our daughter make all of the pickup and drop-off arrangements. Well, one day she was on the phone with her dad and I told her to tell him that I could drop her off at four in the afternoon. There was some discussion, and then she said that I had to drop her off at six. Well, I couldn't do it that late and I didn't understand why her father couldn't take her earlier. I finally called him myself and found out that my daughter wanted to watch a show on television at four-thirty so she told him I couldn't bring her until six. You get the picture."

It's also important not to encourage "spying." Many times parents unintentionally reward the delivery of "confidential" information. For example, what if your child happens to tell you that his mom just broke up with her new boyfriend? Very often, parents urge their child to tell them more by saying things like, "Really? What happened?" or, not so subtly, "Tell me! Who broke up with whom and why!?"

Rewarding the delivery of this kind of information sends the wrong message to your child. You do want to validate your child's possible feelings about the situation he's relating, but you also want to be careful not to encourage him to tell you further "secrets." You might say something that focuses on him rather than on your ex and the situation. For example, if you know he had been having fun with the new boyfriend and now seems disappointed, you can say, "I guess you're a little disappointed about that."

Finally, if you happen to be elated by your ex's misfortune or devastated by his success, leave the room for a moment until you get over it.

"My son and I were building a gingerbread house one Christmas and just as we were attaching the roof, he said, very innocently, 'Daddy and his wife are having a baby." Well, I was so stunned that my hand slipped and knocked down one wall of the house. But I quickly pulled myself together and excused myself, telling him I had to go to the bathroom. Can you imagine how hard it would have been to explain to him what was wrong if I hadn't caught myself?"

No Negative Messages!

Children gain their sense of self from identifying with each parent, so when you criticize your ex, you are, in effect, criticizing your child. Most people can't hide all of their anger all of the time, and children are very perceptive. Don't be surprised to hear your child defend the parent who is being put down, whether she believes the defense or not!

Whereas you may think that your ex is the biggest jerk in the world, your child may feel that your ex is one of the greatest parents, or a least a good person who tries hard. Try to uphold your child's view in front of him and vent to good friends instead.

Although criticizing your ex in front of your child is something you have control over, it may be that he or she doesn't see the need to reciprocate.

"My ex husband is constantly telling our son that women are no good, that they are not to be trusted, that they're gold diggers, etc. I know this for a fact because he felt that way in the marriage. He even says it to me all the time with things like, 'You women are all alike . . .' And, as if I needed further proof, we have a mutual friend who concurs that this is going on.

"I finally brought it up with Steven, our son, and he said that his dad does say those things and he finds it very confusing. I just don't know what to do about it."

Sometimes children do come home with a message like, "Mommy says you're cheap," "Daddy says you're lazy," or, less specifically, "All women are that way" or "Don't ever trust a man." This is actually a good opportunity for an open discussion with your child. You can respond to these statements as if someone other than your ex had said them. Suppose your child came to you and said, "There's a kid at school who says that all women are lazy." You'd probably say to your child, "What do you think about that?" or "Do you think that's true?" or "How do you feel when you hear a statement like that?"

Steven's mother is doing exactly the right thing by talking about her ex's remarks with Steven. If your ex is a true jerk, he or she may not change. The only thing you can do, and the thing you *must* do, is talk to your child about any feelings of being uncomfortable that he might have. Don't approach it as a time to set the record straight, but more as an opportunity for your child to express himself about it. A sample conversation might go like this.

"I often hear your dad say bad things about women, like we're all lazy or we can't be trusted.

"Yeah, he does that a lot."

"Do you believe him? Do you feel that women are one way or another?"

"No, I think women are okay."

"I wonder if it bothers you when your dad starts one of his 'women things'?"

"Yeah, in a way it does. I wish he would just shut up sometimes."

"Do you know that you can tell him what you think about it?"

"Yeah, right, like I'm really going to say something."

"I know it can be hard to approach your dad sometimes. You have good opinions, though, and you're good at being clear about them."

"I guess."

"What else might you do?"

"Well, maybe I could walk away. But what if we're in the car?"

"What do you think would happen if you said something like, 'Please, Dad, can we discuss women at another time,' and left it at that?"

"Maybe. Or maybe I could just ignore him."

"Maybe! I bet you'll think of something that will help you feel more comfortable when he says those things."

It's important to recognize, too, that even though your ex may have said something nasty or off base, an even if your child has relayed the conversation to you "exactly," it could also have lost (or gained) something in the translation. Children often miss a subtle tone of voice, an obvious exaggeration, sarcasm, etc. Knowing that might help you keep your own feelings in check.

Dating Your Child and Other Negative Relationships

In a healthy family, the primary emotional bond is formed and maintained between the parents. Spouses in a healthy marriage do not allow children, grandparents, friends, or anyone else to come between them. Nor do they consistently take sides with these others to form a stronger coalition than the one that exists between themselves. While they might disagree at times, they know that they must consistently back each other up and meet each other's emotional needs first, in order to be able to take care of the other family members.

In many unhealthy marriages (and divorces) this marital bond may be usurped by the children. A primary two-person relationship between a parent and a child can turn into a dangerous situation. If this bond develops in such a way that the parent begins to disclose to the child the feelings he or she would normally share with a spouse, it puts the child in the unhealthy and unfair position of "peer" with the parent. "You're Daddy's only girl now" and "Now that Daddy's gone, you're the man in the family" are classic cases of the parent-child bond.

Putting your child in the role of partner is called "parentifying" and it takes its toll on parents as well as children. For parents, it delays them from getting on with their social lives. Why does Mom need a boyfriend when she has the kids to hang out with? Or how can Dad afford to date when he's got to entertain the kids every weekend?

For children, parentifying gives them an unhealthy amount of responsibility for the parent's emotional well-being and can lead to more problems later on. Children may set out to "cheer Mom up" or to "calm Dad down" when it is not their job to do that.

For many reasons, you may take your time getting back into a dating scene after your divorce. That's up to you, but don't stay away because it's easier (and safer) just to hang out with the kids. Sure, your son may like to go to that movie with you, but instead of just the two of you going, call a friend—one for him and one for you—and make it a foursome.

"A former boyfriend of mine who was a divorced dad once admitted to me that the only intimate emotional relationship he was having was with his daughter. He was a great dad. He was always there for her. But he wasn't there for me."

Parentifying and dating your children have both short- and long-term consequences. In the short term, parentified children may have an exaggerated sense of their own importance, feeling as though they are necessary for Mom or Dad's very survival. In the long term, children who assume too much responsibility for the parent may grow up to resent it and feel deprived of a carefree childhood. They can grow up to be codependent, overly responsible for others, caretakers, rescuers, or incapable of allowing their own needs to be met. These children may also have trouble leaving their parents when they become young adults. In fact, they may never break away from the parent or the need for parental approval. They may have trouble with intimacy because they are afraid that if they get close to someone, they will become responsible for that person.

All families must have clear parent-child boundaries where a parent knows that worrying about where the money is coming from is parent business and worrying about how Santa is going to get down the chimney is kid business. When a child is used as a sounding board for financial fears, or as a confidant for other adult issues, it's overwhelming. By the same token, when a parent spends too much time on the child's level, the child can lack direction and support.

Children in single-parent families may need to take on more responsibilities around the home, but this is not the same thing as parentifying. Children in single-parent families often develop a friendship with the parent, and that isn't bad, as long as the parent's primary need for companionship is met by another adult. As long as clear boundaries exist between the role of the parent and that of the child, with the parent being the leader by providing routines, making decisions, and enforcing and setting limits, the children will be fine.

Don't Encourage Regression

Some parents unintentionally encourage a child's regression or acting out after the divorce, so in effect they can blame the other spouse for this errant behavior. This can be a conscious or a subconscious act. If Tommy, for instance, starts sucking his thumb after the divorce, it could reinforce one parent's view that the divorce was a bad thing.

"My son started having nightmares after the divorce. It made me crazy. I felt so alone on the nights when we

*were up all night battling his imaginary monsters. But
in a way, it also kind of made me feel more important.
Here I was, this divorced dad with a kid who really
needed me. Secretly, I sometimes enjoyed dragging into
work in the morning with bags under my eyes. It made
me feel like I was overcoming these huge burdens."*

If you see your child regressing, get professional help for
both of you. If you can get your ex to see a professional along
with you, that's great, but again, don't ever count on something like that or even waste time saying, "If only he or she
would get help . . ." Get help immediately for you and your
child!

Keep Transition Times Low-Key

The times when your children change homes can be awkward or difficult. Making this transition is a painful reminder
of the reality of the divorce: Mommy or Daddy doesn't live
here anymore. To ease the transition for your child, make as
much of it routine as possible. The child should be told what
time his other parent is coming to pick him up and what exactly will happen when the parent arrives. "When Mom
comes to get you, she'll ring the doorbell and you'll answer
the door. We'll put your things right there, ready to go so you
don't have to hunt for anything. I'll kiss you good-bye and
stand at the door to watch you go."

Likewise, once a child is in her new surroundings, she
may need a period of time to adjust, just as you might when
you arrive at work or return home after a busy day.

"I used to have a terrible time when my child returned home on Sunday nights after spending a weekend with her dad. Crying, tantrums, you name it. Then I realized that as soon as she came home I'd dive right into a project with her. My agenda would be cleaning her room, or making lunch for the next day, something really busy. But what she really needed was just some downtime to adjust to the different dynamics, rules, and routine in our home. So now we take a bath, read a book, and just hug for a while. The tantrums have really lessened because of it."

Keeping transition times low-key means not using them to deliver messages to your ex about late child-support checks or the personal hygiene of your ex's new boyfriend. If your ex tries to bring something up, use your "out" and schedule a time when you'll call to discuss it. The focus during transition should be on your child, not on you and your ex.

Immediately following a transition, you may find that your child has some strong feelings that need to be vented. Allow your child to have those feelings and maybe even brainstorm ways that can make the transition easier.

"My son cried so much on Sunday nights about missing his dad that we finally agreed to have him spend Sunday nights there. His dad now takes him to school on Monday mornings and I pick him up from there. It's worked well for us because I don't have a tired, cranky kid on Sunday nights; school provides the transition he needs, and the bonus is that I see my ex less often!"

Make a Home for Your Child

Imagine having two homes, with some of your things in one place and some of your things in another. Surely you've traveled somewhere and wanted something that you didn't pack. It's not easy for kids who shuttle back and forth.

It's very important for both parents to make room for the child by giving him his own space so he doesn't feel like an intruder. Even if one parent is set up in a studio apartment, it's important to give the child a drawer, a shelf, or a corner as "his." Encourage him to store his things in the space and do what he wants to personalize it. Buy special sheets for his bed that reflect his taste. Perhaps you and your child can decorate the space together, which might involve cutting out images that the child likes from magazines and taping them to a wall. The important thing is that your child feel a sense of "belonging." This is even more important if you're remarried and have other children.

> *"My daughter started complaining that she had to sleep in the hallway at her dad's house, instead of in the bedroom with her half-brother. When I asked him about it, he admitted that his baby had moved out of the crib and now slept in the room with his brother. They had bought a rollaway bed for our daughter, since she slept there only two nights a month. I asked him if he had discussed this with her, and of course he hadn't.*
>
> *"I talked to my daughter about this arrangement and she said she wouldn't mind sleeping in the hallway if it weren't a hallway. We talked about ways she and her dad could somehow fix it up to be her "room." We*

also talked about how she could talk to her dad. She de-
cided that she would do it in person. We practiced an 'I'
message. It went something like, 'Daddy, when I sleep
in the hall I feel lonely and not a part of your family. I'd
like to fix up the hall to be my room.'

"Bless her little heart. She got through to him. I
was ready to jump in and say that she would stop
spending the night if he didn't resolve this. I saved
myself a lot of trouble by letting her handle it. He
eventually put up a door to the hallway and she helped
him paint it a color that she liked—pink, of course."

Form a Council for Cooperation

A very successful parenting tool entails planned meetings
where every family member is present. These "council"
meetings are a place where everyone present has an equal
opportunity to express opinions and feelings, or bring up
problems that haven't been resolved satisfactorily.

The council is, first and foremost, a time you set aside to
discuss important issues. It's helpful to set it for the same
time each week and, preferably, in the same place. In addition, observing certain formalities, like taking notes at each
meeting and following an agenda, gives the meeting some
form and helps those involved know what to expect. Someone should serve as the chairperson and lead the meeting;
you and your child can take turns. Serving as chair provides
a child with an important learning experience that she can
use in the future.

Having an agenda for each meeting ensures that all
issues are heard. During the week, as issues are raised, they

can be written on a piece of paper, which will be brought to the next council. This gives both you and your child some time to collect your thoughts about a particular subject before you enter the discussion phase. Bedtimes, chores, allowances, television viewing are all appropriate subjects. You can also use this time to listen to your child's feelings about the divorce and to figure out ways to make transition times easier on your child.

When you're trying to reach a decision at a council meeting, it's important that you don't vote; you might be outvoted or the result might be a stalemate. It's better to arrive at decisions by way of consensus. Reaching a consensus essentially involves brainstorming, coming up with all the possible solutions to a situation, and then sorting through them until everyone can agree on one. A consensus is sometimes viewed by parents as a difficult process because of the amount of time it takes, especially if the issue is emotional and if there are two very opposing views. But it's worth it. A consensus will save you time in the future, because when two people agree on a specific solution, they're more likely to carry through with it and there will be fewer fights down the line.

One woman said during a workshop we held that she didn't see how she could have "family meetings" when there was only her son and herself. It's important to remember that even if you are a single parent with one child, *you are a family*. Having a family council meeting will send this important message to your child.

The council meetings have many benefits, not the least of which is that they build a sense of cooperation because you are working together on various issues as opposed to separately or individually.

Develop New Rituals

Holidays present problems for most divorced parents, especially during the first year, and will probably always cause some sort of inconvenience, just as juggling two sets of in-laws can for married couples. Religious holidays are often the most difficult, and while Mother's Day and Father's Day are fairly simple, even they can cause problems if you see your child every other weekend and "your" holiday falls on the "other" weekend.

It helps if you can let go of that day as being the only time you can celebrate something. A birthday can be extended to another day or weekend. Mother's Day can last a week, if you design it that way. Then you are free to create a new ritual, which kids love, in a way you want to celebrate.

"I was so upset when my ex wanted my son on Christmas Day, because that's when Santa always came in our family. Upon reflection, however, I discovered that I really didn't like Christmas Day very much. I liked Christmas Eve and Christmas morning but the day and night parts weren't as important to me. What I really wanted to do was get away from all the family and presents and food and just be alone. So I finally told my ex, fine, pick him up at ten, after he opens Santa's presents. I relaxed for a while and then went to a movie. It turned into a great day, and my kid had a great day too!"

Children need to belong to families and groups. They like to have a sense of structure and history. Think of these times not as ones where you can't do what you used to do but as an opportunities to create new rituals that replace the old ones.

Use Trial Periods

If you are hesitant to create a new visitation or holiday schedule with your ex, try it first. There's no law that says a change has to be permanent. But do realize that it's often harder to pull in the reins than to let them out. When you set a precedent, set a trial period along with it: "Let's try this for the next three weeks and then evaluate." Mark it in your calendar, and even if everything is working out fine, in three weeks call your ex as you planned. (If you are in the midst of a big negotiation over visitation or money, check with your lawyer first because you don't want to do something that may come back to haunt you.)

When You Really Can't Stand Your Ex

If you and your ex are at extreme odds, prevent as many meetings, confrontations, and problems as possible. Instead of picking your child up from your ex's house, try to agree that whoever has the child must drop him off at the other's house. It's less territorial, and it tells the child that you approve of the visit and that he's not being taken away but given over. Also, consider a neutral exchange place, like school or a restaurant between both houses.

If you can't stand to be together, even for school and sporting events, arrange to sit on opposite sides of the place.

One mother and father agreed that she would get the right side and he would get the left, just like guests at a wedding, when it came to school auditoriums, ballet recitals, and Little League games. Other parents split up the games and recitals, with one going to dress rehearsal or alternating sporting events.

If you can arrange it, don't share clothes, toys, and other possessions. Give your child his or her own set of things, including pajamas and toothbrush, at your house (or pack a permanent set for the other parent's house, if necessary) so there is less to carry back and forth, less for you to account for and to argue over.

When your child is visiting his other parent, don't call. It can disrupt their time together. Tell your child to call you if she has a need to connect while she is away, and to keep trying if you're not home.

Your Child Has Needs and Rights

It's easy to get caught up in the hassles of the divorce and the battles of custody and forget that your child has needs. She needs to be loved by you for who she is, not for what she does or how she behaves. She needs a relationship with both parents. Because of that relationship, your child needs to be protected from your arguments with your ex. And inclusive of that relationship, your child needs to feel part of a family. This means creating an environment where she feels wanted and welcomed, whether you're the custodial or noncustodial parent.

Your child also has rights. He has the right to experience all of his feelings and thoughts, both positive and negative.

And he has the right to express those feelings and thoughts to you, even if you don't agree with them. Your child has the right to ask questions and receive honest answers from you. Your child has the right to be treated respectfully in all circumstances. This means talking to him in the respectful way that you would talk to another adult, even when you're angry with him.

And finally, your child has the right to and the need for a childhood unburdened by your responsibilities. Walt Disney once said that to a child, every day is like an enormous gift, just waiting to be unwrapped. As parents, we are human, and we make mistakes. But don't make the mistake of squashing that gift.

11

Living on the
Bright Side

Take a Tip from the Pilot

Every day, some 750,000 Americans hear words that could save their lives and the lives of their children, and they barely take notice of them. This important information is announced during the takeoff of every commercial airplane flight in America. The pilot says, "If the cabin loses pressure, an oxygen mask will drop down in front of you. Place the mask over *your* mouth and tighten the straps *before* you attempt to help your child or anyone else." Think about this for a minute. This procedure makes sense. In a crisis, we function better if we take care of *our* immediate needs first. Then we are equipped to help others.

This means that you are allowed to take the time to heal after your divorce. And it means that you are allowed to do what feels right for yourself. If that means hiring a baby-sitter to get away from the kids one night, making a phone call to a sympathetic friend before making an important decision, or going for a long drive into the sunset, do it!

Time Takes Time

Dealing with the complexities of life after divorce can sometimes make you feel as though you'll never get past it. As one person said, "I know I need to take care of myself better. It's just that I feel like I'm constantly picking up the pieces of disasters and that I don't have time even to stop to think, much less take time out for me. And yet I know if I did it would make things easier to begin with."

Keep in mind that over time, things change. It may be hard right now, but nothing lasts forever.

"We separated right after my daughter was born. My ex and I talked, argued, negotiated on every bit of parenting. When to feed her, which play group she should go to, where she should go to school, homework, you name it. But as she got older, we talked less, just because the

seeds we had planted, so to speak, had grown into a beautiful garden. We have a gorgeous daughter who will graduate from college soon. My ex is still a jerk about some things, but our contact is minimal compared to what it used to be."

Developing a compatible relationship with your ex may take longer than your marriage. But don't give up. Give yourself time to recover from the emotional turmoil by learning to treat yourself well. Taking the dog for a walk (even if you don't have a dog) can change your mindset and clear your thoughts. Hot baths, good books, long movies, and exercise can help get you through the hard times.

There is life after divorce. As a matter of fact, many people go on to live happily ever after. Of course, some never seem to get over the hurt, anger, and devastation. The difference between these two types of people lies in whether they've taken the time to help themselves and to make educated choices and learn from those choices along the way.

Balance Is a Key to Calm Living

Just as a balanced diet helps you maintain a healthy body, a balanced lifestyle brings a sense of order and proportion. It is the yin and yang of Zen, the good and bad, the old and new.

As you carve out your new "jerk-free" lifestyle, look to balance it with equal parts of work and play, with giving and receiving, with thoughts and feelings. Beware of excess and neglect. When you feel yourself going down the path of extremes, stop for a moment and look around. A balanced lifestyle gives you the freedom to attain new goals and to experience peace of mind and body.

Today Is Only One Day

There may be days when your ex exasperates you so much that you can think of nothing else. Thoughts of revenge fill your mind and cloud your thinking. As you lie around wondering why you don't have the energy to find the remote control to change the television station, remember that these feelings won't last forever. These are the very natural feelings of grief and loss. And you must allow yourself to grieve. It's been said that tears are to the soul what soap is to the body. Be aware, too, that although pain is sometimes inevitable, suffering is often optional.

Acknowledging your grief and loss and moving through it will keep it from lingering deep inside of you and resurfacing to sabotage your new relationships or your continuing relationship with your ex.

Some people have found it helpful to have a list of things to do during these times. They keep it tucked away in a special place. Put little jobs on the list that bring immediate rewards, like polishing silver or doing a load of laundry. If you don't have the energy to clean your entire apartment, it's enough to do just the dishes or to empty the garbage during this distressing time. You may not have the energy to run five miles, but a walk around the block can clear the fog from your brain. And maybe you don't have time for that round of golf, but how about hitting a bucket of balls at the local driving range? Or buying that magazine that suddenly appeals to you and finding a quiet bench or coffee bar to read it? And pat yourself on the back for being able to do just one little positive thing for yourself.

> *"After we split up, I moved into my own apartment. It was so depressing at first. I could afford only a one-bedroom apartment and I wanted to have a bed for Ben when he came on weekends, so I ended up getting two twin beds. I hadn't slept in a twin since college.*
>
> *"Anyway, I was always depressed whenever I walked into the bedroom. Plus it was a mess, with clothes all over the place. Then a friend suggested that I decorate it. She went with me to buy sheets and curtains and blankets, in all these great-looking colors.*
>
> *"After that, I started making the bed each day and changing the sheets each week. I couldn't believe the difference this made. I even arranged the beds so that I could push them together to look like a king-sized bed when Ben wasn't there. Now, when I'm feeling sad about being single, I change the sheets to give the room a different look. It helps a lot."*

Encourage Each Other

Take the time to encourage your child and yourself. A little encouragement can go a long way, and encouragement builds upon itself. A few kind words may be just what you need to get you through the difficult times. Be your own best friend and acknowledge to yourself those things you've done right today. And remember to encourage your child. Encouraging words help people feel closer to each other, and you'll be surprised to see that your child will pick up on your encouragement and give you a few encouraging words of her own.

Take the Time to Make New Friends

Terence Gorski, in *Getting Love Right*, believes that to attract a quality partner we must become a quality person. And if we have had bad luck with relationships, we need to do something to change that. We need to practice relationship-building skills just as we would practice a golf swing or the piano. He believes that you can develop relationship skills only by being in a relationship.

Because of your divorce, you most likely feel lonely for a friend, a sexual companion, a parenting partner, or a family network. These are all very natural results of the upheaval you've been through.

For this reason, it's important to seek out other single parents to spend time with as adults and as parents, to share in some of the work, and to help each other when you can. It's helpful and reassuring to know that you're not the only one in the boat.

Finding Things You Like to Do— And Doing Them

Reentering the social scene after your divorce may feel akin to jumping into an ocean of sharks. Keep in mind that there are many ways to meet people. Some people enroll in adult education classes, take up a hobby, enter bikeathons or walkathons. Others tell their friends that they'd like to meet single people. Trying some of these will soon have you meeting people, having fun, and forgetting that your ex is a jerk.

Don't Look for a Diamond in a Bag of Coal

Getting rid of your expectations about your ex also helps you move forward. If your ex was unable to meet your needs during your marriage, he won't be able to meet them now. If you look for a diamond in the coal bin or shop for apples at the hardware store, you'll feel disappointed, dissatisfied, and discontent.

Your ex is not going to change. The goal here is to have a great life anyway. You can still find happiness, whether your ex is acting like a jerk or a responsible person.

> *"After we split up, I went on to become a therapist and specialized in marriage counseling. Everything was fine until my ex remarried, had a few kids, and didn't have enough money to go around. He turned into a real jerk about child support and we wound up in court. He kept wanting to know what my boyfriend contributed to our living expenses so that he could claim I needed less support. Every time he brought this up, I saw red. We had struck a bargain ten years before on a set amount. I wasn't asking for more. What my boyfriend contributed was my business.*
>
> *"After a particularly grueling day in court, I started beating up on myself, thinking here I am, a*

therapist who's supposed to know how couples commu-
nicate, and my ex and I haven't been speaking for six
months.

"That night, I went out with my boyfriend and child
to a movie that I really wanted to see. I couldn't pay at-
tention to the movie. I just kept thinking about what
had gone on in court. How could he say such a thing,
why didn't I say this, I wish I hadn't said that, he's a
jerk and a liar. Then it hit me. As long as I let this go
on in my head, he was winning. He had the power.
Once I put it out of my mind, I could relax and get on
with my life. I could still be angry at him, as long as I
didn't take it out on my kid or kick the dog. I could also
let it go. My ex is going to do what he is going to do re-
gardless of me. I had a choice. I could forget about him
and enjoy the movie or I could stew. The movie was
great!"

When you sit and ruminate about your ex's behavior, you
are voluntarily giving away your power. While it may be hard
to think about anything else (especially at first), try some alternative input, like getting together with a friend or renting
a movie. Otherwise you may stay glued to your unhappiness
for a long, long time.

"I couldn't believe this single mom I was dating. I had
rented a ski house. It was the weekend before the season
started, and I didn't have my son and she didn't have
hers, so I had the house all to myself. When I called her
and invited her out for the weekend, she said yes. But
then on Friday she called and told me that she had
gotten a letter from her ex's lawyer and was really
upset. She canceled our weekend, saying that she really

wanted to spend the time drafting a response to his letter. I couldn't believe it. She chose to blow off a weekend in the mountains for a letter to her ex. That was the last time I ever asked her out. I heard recently, too, that three years later, she's still not divorced."

Seeing the Positive Side of Things

If we make the most of what we have, we will have more. While it's often difficult to see the positive side of things, taking the time to practice looking at things positively increases your ability to do so. It's like going to the gym to get stronger. You begin with light weights, practice a little each day, and get stronger and stronger. Looking at the glass as half full instead of half empty just takes a little practice each day. You do have a choice about how to look at things. If you choose to look at life negatively, you produce more negative energy and your life becomes more negative. When you choose to look at things positively, that positive energy attracts more positive energy, which can be used for growth. Instead of seeing yourself as a part of a broken home, see yourself as a solid family.

Using Your Positive Affirmations

We cannot emphasize enough the power of the positive affirmations you learned reading this book. They are one of the most effective ways to bring about positive changes in your life. Turning negative phrases like "It will never work" into positive ones like "Let's give it a try" opens doors and creates opportunities. Here again it becomes your choice to get on with a better life or to wallow in self-pity. Turn "It's a waste of time" into "Think of the possibilities." Change "I don't know what to do" into "I have so many choices." Soon you'll be hearing yourself say, "Yeah, my ex used to make me crazy and he still acts like a jerk sometimes. But I've got better things to do than waste my time and energy on him."

Forgiveness Is Empowering

Your ex may have done things or said things to you during and after your marriage that you feel very unforgiving about. You can't change history, but you can change your attitude about it. Forgiveness doesn't mean that you approve of what your ex did or didn't do. It means that you no longer want to dwell on it or remember it every time you speak to or see your ex. Think of the energy that recalling the past zaps right out of your body. You have the option of putting that energy to use in a more positive way.

Forgiving your ex is not the same as letting him or her off the hook. It's akin to cutting the line. It's an act that frees you of your ex. When you forgive your ex, you literally let go of the past instead of being dragged along by it. Letting go of your anger lightens your heart and loosens your emotional ties to your ex.

Keeping Your Sense of Humor

Abraham Lincoln once said, "Most people are as happy as they make up their minds to be."

A sense of humor isn't something that's taught. It's something that's chosen and developed. It's allowed to emerge and encouraged to appear. There is humor in every situation if you look hard enough. Someone once said that humor is like looking at three sides to a coin. Robin Williams has been quoted as saying that it's like acting out optimism. When you find humor in your situation, you feel lighter and brighter.

Laughter itself allows you to forget your troubles, if only for a moment. Milton Berle called it "an instant vacation." Kurt Vonegut once said, "The biggest laughs are based on the biggest disappointments and the biggest fears." Perhaps you can find a laugh from the disappointing time you've been through or muster a chuckle about your fears of the future. Laughter, indeed humor itself, is like a muscle. It gets stronger if you use it and atrophies if you don't.

Enjoy yourself. Before you know it, the kids will be off to college and your interaction with your ex will diminish. Over time, your ex may even turn out to be an okay person, because of your new positive attitude and direct communication techniques.

And Finally . . .

Instead of dwelling on what you don't have, take a good look at what you do have. You are family. Whether you number two or ten, you're a family. And being in a family, no matter what its size or shape, is special.

Bibliography

Ahrons, Constance R., Ph.D. *The Good Divorce—Keeping Your Family Together When Your Marriage Comes Apart*. New York: HarperCollins, 1994.

Al-Anon Family Group Headquarters. *Courage To Change*. New York: Al-Anon Family Group Headquarters, 1992.

Bauer, Jill. *From I Do to I'll Sue*. New York: Penguin, 1993.

Beattie, Melody. *The Language of Letting Go*. San Francisco: Harper Hazeldon, 1990.

Belli, Melvin, and Mel Krantzler. *The Complete Guide to Men and Women Divorcing*. New York: St. Martin's Press, 1988.

Berger, Stuart, M.D. *Divorce Without Victims: Helping Children Through Divorce With a Minimum of Pain and Trauma*. New York: Signet, 1986.

Biddulph, Steve and Shaaron. *The Secret of a Happy Family*. New York: Bantam, 1988.

Blau, Melinda. *Families Apart: Ten Keys to Successful Co-Parenting*. New York: Putnam, 1994.

Bradshaw, John. *Bradshaw On: The Family*. Deerfield Beach, Fla.: Health Communications, 1988.

Clarke, Jean Illsley. *Self-Esteem: A Family Affair*. San Francisco: Winston Press, 1978.

Cohen, Marion Galpher. *The Joint Custody Handbook*. Philadelphia: Running Press, 1991.

Covey, Stephen R. *The Seven Habits of Highly Effective People*. New York: Simon & Schuster, 1989.

Feinberg, Mortimer, Ph.D., and John J. Tarrant. *Why Smart People Do Dumb Things*. New York: Fireside, 1995.

Garrity, Carla, and Mitchell Baris. *Caught in the Middle: Protecting the Children of High-Conflict Divorce*. Lexington, Mass.: D.C. Heath, 1994.

Gorski, Terence T. *Getting Love Right*. New York: Fireside/Parkside, 1993.
———. *Keeping the Balance* . Independence, Mo.: Herald House, 1993.

Gray, John. *Men Are From Mars, Women Are From Venus*. New York: Harper Collins, 1992.

Hendrix, Harville, Ph.D. *Getting the Love You Want*. New York: HarperCollins, 1990.

Jeffers, Susan, Ph.D. *Feel the Fear and Do It Anyway.* New York: Fawcett Columbine, 1987.

Jewett, C. *Helping Children Cope With Separation and Loss.* Boston: Harvard Common, 1982.

Jolin, Peter G. *How to Succeed as a Stepparent.* New York: Signet, 1981.

Keenan, Barbara Mullen. *When You Marry a Man With Children.* New York: Pocket Books, 1992.

Kennedy, Marge, and Janet Spencer King. *The Single-Parent Family: Living Happily in a Changing World.* New York: Crown, 1994.

Krantzler, Mel. *Creative Divorce.* New York: Signet, 1975.

Lansky, Vicki. *Vickie Lansky's Divorce Book for Parents.* New York: Penguin, 1989.

Lofas, Jeanette, and Dawn B. Sova. *Step-Parenting.* New York: Zebra Books, 1985.

Marston, Stephanie. *The Divorced Parent: Success Strategies for Raising Your Children After Separation.* New York: William Morrow, 1994.

Nelsen, Jane, Cheryl Erwin, and Carol Delzer. *Positive Discipline for Single Parents: A Practical Guide to Raising Children Who Are Responsible, Respectful and Resourceful.* Rockland, Calif.: Prima Publishing, 1994.

Paris, Eran. *Step-Families: Making Them Work.* New York: Avon, 1984.

Peck, Dr. M. Scott. *Further Along The Road Less Traveled.* New York: Simon & Schuster, 1993.

———. *The Road Less Traveled.* New York: Touchstone, 1978.

Popkin, Michael. *Active Parenting.* New York: Harper & Row, 1987.

Ricci, Isolina. *Mom's House, Dad's House: Making Shared Custody Work.* New York: Macmillan, 1980.

Ross, Julie A. *Practical Parenting For the 21st Century: The Manual You Wish Had Come With Your Child.* New York: Excalibur Publishing, 1993.

Samalin, Nancy, with Martha Moraghan Jablow. *Loving Your Child Is Not Enough.* New York: Penguin, 1987.

Samalin, Nancy, with Catherine Whitney. *Love And Anger: The Parental Dilemma.* New York: Penguin, 1991.

Shechtman, Morris R. *Working Without a Net: How to Survive and Thrive in Today's High Risk Business World.* New York: Pocket Books, 1994.

Smalley, Gary, and John Trent. *Love Is a Decision.* Dallas: World Publishing, 1989.

———. *The Language of Love.* Colorado Springs: Focus on the Family Publishing, 1988.

Smedes, Louis B. *Forgive and Forget*. New York: Pocket Books, 1984.

Smith, Manuel, Ph.D. *When I Say No, I Feel Guilty*. New York: Bantam, 1975.

Spence, Gerry. *How to Argue and Win Every Time*. New York: St. Martin's Press, 1995.

Tannen, Deborah, Ph.D. *You Just Don't Understand*. New York: Ballantine, 1990.

Tavris, Carol. *Anger*. New York: Touchstone, 1982.

Teyber, Edward. *Helping Children Cope With Divorce*. Lexington, Mass.: D.C. Heath, 1992.

Ury, William. *Getting Past No: Negotiating Your Way From Confrontation to Cooperation*. New York: Bantam, 1991.

Virtue, Doreen. *My Kids Don't Live With Me Anymore: Coping with the Custody Crisis*. Minneapolis: CompCare Publishers, 1988.

Wallerstein, Judith S., and Sandra Blakeslee. *The Good Marriage*. Boston: Houghton Mifflin, 1995.